BUT WHERE WERE THE BLUEBIRDS?

First published in 2010 by

WOODFIELD PUBLISHING LTD
West Sussex ~ England ~ PO21 5EL
www.woodfieldpublishing.co.uk

© Patricia Bending, 2010

All rights reserved.
No part of this publication may be reproduced
or transmitted in any form or by any means,
electronic or mechanical, nor may it be stored
in any information storage and retrieval system,
without prior permission from the publisher.

The right of Patricia Bending
to be identified as Author of this work
has been asserted in accordance with
the Copyright, Designs and Patents Act 1988

ISBN 1-84683-091-5

But Where Were the Bluebirds?

A child's-eye view of the 1940s

To Amy with love and all good wishes

PATRICIA BENDING

Patricia Bending

Woodfield

Woodfield Publishing Ltd

Interesting and informative books on a variety of subjects

For full details of all our published titles, visit our website at
www.woodfieldpublishing.co.uk

*for my grandchildren
and anyone who has wondered what it was like
– and anyone who remembers…*

"The Second World War produced, in the end,
one victor, the United States,
one hero, Great Britain,
one villain, Germany."

('Hitler' by N. Stone)

~ CONTENTS ~

Acknowledgements .... *ii*

Introduction .... *iii*

1. "The Day War Broke Out…" ~ 1939/40 1
2. "We're On Our Own Now" ~ 1940 10
3. "It's a Bomber's Moon Tonight!" ~ 1940 18
4. The 2nd Great Fire of London ~ 1940/41 27
5. "London Can Take It" ~ 1941 34
6. "Don't You Know There's a *War* on?" ~ 1941 42
7. "Yes! We Have No Bananas" 48
8. "It's That Man Again!" 57
9. Land of Hope and Glory 63
10. The Big Three ~ 1941/42 69
11. Yankee Doodle Dandy ~ 1943/44 77
12. I Knew Hitler's Name But He Didn't Know Mine ~ 1944/45 83
13. Where Were the Bluebirds? ~ 1945 90
14. Aftermath ~ 1945 97
15. The Beginning of the Cold War ~ 1946 102
16. The New World Order ~ 1947 109
17. Growing Up In A Changing World ~ 1948 117
18. Another New Word, 'Teenager' ~ 1949/50 122
19. A Visit to Franco's Spain ~ 1950/51 130
20. London Belongs to Me! ~ 1951-53 136

Looking Back *143*

Appendix I ~ Tadek's Story *145*

Appendix II ~ A Word on the British Empire *148*

But Where Were the Bluebirds? ~ i

Acknowledgements

In the early stages of researching the historical background for this book, my first thanks must be to the BBC, whose television documentaries about WWII have, for me, been particularly informative and those about the Home Front often nostalgic.

In addition I must thank the authors of the following books, from which I have used quotations for further information:

Invasion 1940 by Peter Fleming. Hamish Hamilton 1958.

The City That Wouldn't Die by Richard Collier. Collins 1959.

The Secret War by Brian Johnson. BBC Publications 1978.

Wartime and Aftermath by Bernard Bergonzi. Oxford University Press 1993.

Blitz by M J Gaskin. Faber and Faber 2005.

After the Victorians by A N Wilson. Hutchinson 2005.

Empire: How Britain Made the Modern World by Niall Ferguson. The Penguin Group 2007.

I also owe a great debt to family and friends: my elder sister Barbara and elder brother Frank, who have contributed their own memories; George, my old friend remembered fondly, whose knowledge of history kept our conversations always interesting and who was the inspiration for writing this book; my son-in-law, Adrian, a historian, who read and re-read many drafts ensuring dates and events were accurate; my eldest son, Stephen, who patiently sat instructing me on computers and improving old photos; Paul, my youngest son, whose interest in our family history and roots kept me engaged in this project; and my daughter, Christina, who has spent many hours sourcing official photographs and obtaining permissions for use, and without whom the book would have never got to the publishing stage.

Lastly, I am very grateful to have found a delightful publisher of this genre who has patiently waited for the *actual, final, complete* version!

Introduction

"The Past is a foreign country: they do things differently there."
L.P. Hartley (1895-1972)

If you look at a map of the world, the two islands of Britain and Ireland appear to be leaning towards each other in a 'together' sort of way. Certainly when I was at primary school in the 1940s, both my Dad and my teacher were still referring to them together as 'the British Isles' even though Eire had broken away from the British Crown in the 1920s. It took a while to become used to saying 'the United Kingdom' instead.

I heard the adults around me using the everyday terms of 'the British Isles' and 'Great Britain' at the same time as the Second World War was spreading around the globe. A big proportion of the school's world map on our classroom wall was coloured pink to denote the countries of the British Empire and Commonwealth, our family of nations, our friends and Allies. The Enemy was 'Jerry' – unseen and threatening.

Looking back now, it all seems like a story book. Even the familiar names, heard so often in conversation and on the BBC News, have become characters in history books or historical fiction. Yet, as a young child, I took for granted the wartime world as I found it, mainly apprehended by family jokes or grumbles about the tiresome aspects of civilian life – sometimes spiced with fear or dread, but always adding zest to my childish joy of being alive.

I know that others before me have recorded their memories of growing up in the 1940s, but late in life I thought – as one of the youngest and possibly the last! – that I would put down my own before there is no-one left to give an eye-witness account, albeit from the viewpoint of a child, of living in that 'foreign country' of the past, during and in the years immediately following, one of the most vivid periods of our history, when heroism, romance, tragedy and humour were all entwined.

This is my story of growing up in Enfield, north London (with a year in Cuffley, Hertfordshire), during the 1940s, beginning with my fifth birthday at the beginning of the war and ending when I started work in the early 1950s. I have based it upon a kaleidoscopic collection of fragments of memory, which I have tried to set, more or less in order of sequence, against the background of wartime events and the global changes of the postwar years.

Cuffley, Monday 28th [Aug 1939]

Dear Mother,

I received your card this morning as we arrived home earlier than expected. I had written but to Vista Avenue because I thought you would return because of the crisis. There is much excitement here it's even more serious than September [sic]. London children are evacuating again and all valuable things are being removed and buried. Museums etc are closed.

You didn't mention crisis on the card so I thought perhaps you have not been having papers. If I were you I should buy them. Hitler is demanding his last territorial claim in Europe once more – Danzig. Envoys are flying from Berlin to London and vice versa and to crown all Russia has made a pact to help Germany.

A few days ago civilians were asked to carry their gas masks with them and so I was going home to get mine but you are still away. Auntie Nellie, Clem and Edna took theirs away with them. I don't know whether Mrs Jenkins has the key – I expect so, but you could send a card to tell me.

Perhaps this will all blow over as before, let us hope so, but it's best to be ready. We went up to town Saturday and Auntie Nellie got some stores of tins and goods and black curtaining. The Civil Service Food Dept. was packed.

We had a portable wireless while we were away because Clem and Ed had to keep in touch with the news, so we were in touch with civilisation.

I am sorry I didn't write sooner but I have really written lots of cards and then we moved miles away from villages and I couldn't post them.

I hope you like it at St Osyth and are enjoying yourselves. Perhaps the weather on the east coast is better than it was in Scotland. We saw every kind of weather – scorching sun, pouring rain, thunder and it was often icy cold – even saw snow.

Well, I had better say goodbye. I think Auntie Nellie will write to you. I hope you will not have to come home before the 2nd but keep in touch with the news. It isn't very encouraging and the east coast isn't particularly safe.

Give my love to Auntie Louie and Nana and Mr Todd when they come.

Best wishes, Barbara

PS Writing a bit queer but I am writing on my knee.

I think perhaps you had better come home. We have just heard that the people are being evacuated instead of the said rehearsal. Everything looks black and even if it's all right it's better to be home. Auntie Nellie thinks it would be better. Parliament is meeting tomorrow – goodness knows what will happen then. Just going home to get my mask, hoping Mrs. J has got the key.

We keep hearing lots of news and war's inevitable. Then we think it's all right.

Love, Barbara XXX

PS If anything happens the trains will be very crowded so it's best to be home soon.

Letter to Mum from 15-year-old Barbara, 1939.

1. "The Day War Broke Out…" ~ 1939/40

We left the grown-ups behind – they just wanted to sit there and talk about a man called Hitler. All I cared about was that today was my 5th birthday *(30th August 1939)* and I was having a wonderful time at the seaside with my big brother Frank (aged 11), building sandcastles and paddling in the tiny waves.

We were staying in a wooden bungalow with a verandah right on the beach *(at St. Osyth on the East Coast)*. Nana (my grandmother) was here for the day with her new husband Mr Todd (who was *very* old with a big grey moustache) and her sister Auntie Louie, my favourite auntie, plump and cuddly. They all called me Patsy.

In the evening I heard Mum and Dad talking to the others about a letter from my big sister Barbara (aged 15), urging us to go home. Barbara had been on holiday with our cousin Clement and his wife Edna, touring Scotland in a caravan, but now they were back at Clem's house in Cuffley *(Hertfordshire)*. Barbara's letter was all about the news on the wireless *(radio)* and she thought the East Coast was not particularly safe! I wondered why, but I knew it was no good asking. Grown-ups were always telling me not to ask so many questions.

The BBC News reported the latest territorial demands of Adolf Hitler (Chancellor of Germany and leader of the NAZIS – National Socialist Party); the mobilization of British troops; the removal to safer locations of national treasures from London's museums and art galleries; and so on… Hitler had already seized control of Austria and Czechoslovakia and made a secret pact with Stalin (President and dictator of the USSR – Union of Soviet Socialist Republics) to share in the conquest of Poland, a nation to which Great Britain had given a guarantee of protection.

Next day Mum and Dad started tidying up in the bungalow and Frank and I went out to play on the beach for the last time. The hot sand was burning our bare feet so we ran down to the edge of the sea, where there was a line of jellyfish that had been stranded by the tide. Frank pretended he was going to chop one in half with his spade and I screamed at him, "Don't!"

That night there was a violent storm, the sea lit up with lightning. In bed I lay listening to the thunder and was glad we were going home in the morning.

On Friday, 1st September 1939, German troops invaded Poland.

Mum and Dad took us back to London on the train. We lived in Vista Avenue, Brimsdown *(in the Enfield borough on the northern edge of London).*

It was good to be home again with my own things. There was a swing in the back garden, or I could ride on my tricycle; and when Frank wasn't around I could take his marbles out into the street and roll them along the pavement, hoping someone would come along to play with me.

When Dad handed out my regular 'Saturday Penny' Frank took me along to the sweet-shop on the corner. On the shelves were jars of barley-sugar twists, butterscotch, 'cough drops' (golden-brown boiled sweets flavoured with liquorice and aniseed) and liquorice allsorts. After some argument with Frank, I settled for Sherbet powder in a little paper bag with a hollow liquorice tube to dip into it. Frank got a packet of ten 'cigarettes' (little white sugar sticks stained deep pink at one end), so that we could pretend to smoke like the grown-ups.

At the end of the cul-de-sac where we lived there was a stony lane leading to some open scrubby land. Frank sometimes took me there to play with Vernon, the boy next door. Vernon's house always smelt 'doggy' because his mother bred big Newfoundland dogs for showing at Crufts – her neighbours on the other side let her have the use of their garden for kennels. *(Vernon Handley became known in later life as one of the conductors of the London Philharmonic Orchestra and I saw him when he conducted 'the Last Night of the Proms.')*

There was an airfield not far away and I was used to hearing aeroplanes flying over our house. Frank told me they were Spitfires. I was on my own in the garden, practising my new-found trick of turning head-over-heels, when I heard a plane that sounded different from usual and stopped to look up. There it was, moving across the sky, but much too slowly, with the engine stuttering, coming back to life and dying away again. I stared up with growing alarm. PLEASE God don't let it fall out of the sky! Then the engine cut out altogether and I held my breath.

Everything seemed to happen in slow motion, the plane suspended in silence, nose dipping, beginning to fall straight down and to spin round and round. Before it could reach the ground, I jumped up and fled indoors to the kitchen. Mum was just standing at the sink, peeling potatoes – she didn't *know*! I worried for an instant whether I should tell her, then thought, Better Not! *(Looking back, this must have been a Spitfire pilot practising aerobatics.)*

After supper, I took up my usual position at the front room window, anxious not to miss the lamplighter. He always appeared at twilight and I liked watching him go along the street with his long pole, lighting up the gas lamp-posts one by one. But this time I was disappointed. The street got darker and darker and I wondered why he didn't come. Then Mum called me off to bed. *(I never saw the lamplighter again.)*

In the morning, coming in from the back garden for a drink of water, I was a bit put out to find the kitchen empty. Why wasn't Mum cooking the dinner? I heard a voice in the front room and went in to have a look. Mum, Dad and Frank were all in there, listening to a man on the wireless making a speech in a very solemn voice. Mum gave me a sharp look, so I drifted outside again, feeling a bit cross. Usually it was all jokes and laughter when Dad was at home and I just hoped the day would soon get back to normal.

Just then I heard a strange wailing noise in the distance. Frank came to the back door and called for me to come inside and the noise went on and on, rising up and down. I was curious, remembering an expression I'd once heard – the Wailing Banshee. Was this a Wailing Banshee?

At 11 o'clock on Sunday morning, 3rd September 1939, Prime Minister Neville Chamberlain spoke to the nation on the wireless: "…I have to tell you now … this country is at war with Germany."

A short while later, people heard the Air Raid Warning, but it proved to be a false alarm, set off by an unidentified plane crossing our coastline, and was almost immediately followed by the All Clear.

Frank stopped me from going into the front room. He said Mum was crying but he wouldn't tell me why. Then, in a few minutes, Dad came out, saying, "Let's have a cup of tea," so I cheered up straightaway because that meant everything was all right again.

Later, on my way to play in the street outside, I heard Mum and Dad arguing. They were in the front room again and the door was closed, so I stopped outside to listen.

"I'm not having my children taken away," Mum declared. "We'll stay together and take our chance." She got very excited and said, "If a bomb falls on us we might as well all go together!"

I tiptoed off as fast as I could before they caught me by the door. Thank goodness I wasn't going to be sent away. Nothing else could be half as terrible. I decided then and there, if there was any choice in the matter, I wanted to stay at home with the family – never mind about a bomb!

At the beginning of September 1939, more than 1,500,000 children were evacuated from London and other cities to safer places in the country. They were billeted with families in villages or farms, brothers and sisters staying together if possible. Most schools moved teachers and children 'en masse' and re-established themselves wherever they could find space. Many older children looked on it all as a great adventure – one trainload from the East End of London departed singing, The Lambeth Walk! But there were tears from the younger ones when they had to leave their mothers behind. Only mothers with young babies were evacuated together.

The King and Queen saw it as their duty to 'remain at their post' and they kept the two young princesses, Elizabeth and Margaret, with them in London.

In the evening I was very curious when I saw Dad fixing up what he called 'plywood panels' over the windows. "Why is Dad doing that?" Dad didn't hear me, but Mum said, "Well … there are some wicked men about and we don't want them to see our lights." I froze, terrified. I'd always thought that Wicked Men, like Ogres, belonged only in storybooks. Why were Wicked Men looking for *us?* Another of those mysteries which grown-ups never explained. But nothing terrible happened and next morning everybody was carrying on as usual. Perhaps Wicked Men could only come out in the dark…?

My big sister was still in Cuffley with Clem and Edna, not far from Clem's mother, Auntie Nellie, who lived in a big house further up the hill. I heard Dad talking to Mum about going to stay with Auntie Nellie *(his brother's widow)* for the 'Duration' – a mysterious new word. Mum said Auntie Nellie would probably prefer us rather than unknown 'evacuees'.

The family packed up – they took no notice of my half-hearted protests – and we set off for Cuffley. I was not at all sure whether this was a Good Thing. As the youngest, I was indulged by all the family and I didn't want that happy state of affairs to come to an end. The trouble was that Auntie Nellie expected children to behave themselves. I'd heard her say that children should be Seen and Not Heard!

Still, I was very impressed by her big, comfortable house with its long garden. And, best of all, she had a wooden chest *(ottoman)* against the wall of the living room which, when you raised the lid, revealed a lot of interesting toys. There was a lovely little yellow giraffe with long black eyelashes; big picture books; jigsaw puzzles; and a board coloured to look like a farm, farmyard and surrounding fields with tiny models of the farmhouse, barns, haystacks, cows and chickens.

So long as I made sure to keep out of Auntie Nellie's way, I thought I'd be able to have a jolly good time here. After all, we'd only come for the Duration – whatever that might be – so we must be going home some time.

Auntie Nellie didn't have to put plywood over the windows at night. She had very heavy, thick black curtains hanging outside the ordinary curtains, both drawn together when it got dark, so nobody could see the lights from outside.

The grown-ups still went on talking about Hitler and War. Auntie Nellie said she was with Barbara at Clem's house on the day war was declared and they'd all got very alarmed when the Air Raid Warning went off. Clem decided they should stay in the kitchen. Then he suddenly thought of a gas attack and fetched a blanket, which he soaked in water and hung over the door and window. Edna switched off the Sunday roast . . . a few aircraft flew over . . . the All Clear sounded . . . and Sunday dinner was rather late!

Barbara was still in Clem's house but, after some mysterious words from Auntie Nellie about 'Doing her Bit', three boys turned up to live with us. Barbara told me later that someone had called to ask whether we could take an evacuee from London's East End, so Auntie Nellie was expecting only one and got a bit of a shock when *three* arrived. There were two brothers, Ernest and Terry, aged eight and five, and a bigger boy, Ian, aged eleven.

That night Frank and I were put to bed upstairs, together with the three boys, all in a row across an enormous double bed. We scuffled, pushed and giggled and generally larked about until we finally ended up singing:

> *There were five in a bed and the little one said,*
> *'Roll over. Roll over.'*
> *They all rolled over and one fell out.*
> *There were four in a bed and the little one said ...*

Auntie Nellie called the boys 'the Young Scamps'. I got the feeling I was included in this description. Someone in the family always said, "Here comes Trouble," whenever I appeared on the scene.

Barbara and Frank had to go back to school.

Following declaration of war, schools, cinemas and theatres had all been closed down, but were slowly returning to normal.

Grown-ups never told *me* anything, but it turned out that moving to Cuffley meant Mum didn't have to worry about her children being evacuated. It so happened that Frank's school was also evacuated to Cuffley. Barbara's school was considered to be in a 'Safe Area' on the western side of Enfield and Barbara could get there by train from Cuffley to Enfield Chase.

Frank was known at his school as the only 'private evacuee' living with his family and he told me later that he got some stick for this from the other boys – nor did his teacher treat him very kindly!

The rest of us were free to run wild outdoors until it got dark and most days we spent exploring in the woods further down the road. The boys disappeared into the trees and I had to run after them. Like any boy I'd ever met they thought girls were soppy, but Terry, the youngest, always had a friendly grin. We climbed trees, played hide-and-seek or Cowboys and Indians. We set off to be intrepid explorers, hacking our way through the jungle. Sometimes we got lost in the woods and were late getting home. Then we had to face the music!

We all sat round the table while Auntie Nellie dished up. We didn't much like the greens, but you had to eat your greens or go without pudding and we all wanted the bread-and-butter pudding – thin slices of buttered bread, sprinkled with sultanas, covered with custard and baked in the oven.

Dad kept on talking about a 'phoney war' – nothing much seemed to be happening. And one day, much to my disappointment, the three evacuees went home. I supposed they were homesick, especially as Christmas was coming.

'Phoney' was the word used by the Americans to describe the first few months of the war – but it was hardly a phoney war for the Poles. The Germans bombed Warsaw, invading their country and ruthlessly suppressed all Polish resistance, aided and abetted by Russian troops from the east.

Nor was it a phoney war in the Battle of the Atlantic. On the day war was declared, a German submarine had torpedoed the British outward-bound passenger liner Athenia, which sank with the loss of 125 lives, including those of 28 Americans fleeing home. Two weeks later, another enemy submarine torpedoed and sank the Royal Navy's aircraft carrier Courageous, with the loss of more than 500 of her crew.

With no evacuees to play with, I had to spend more time with the grown-ups. At least I could listen to their conversation. They said much more interesting things to each other than they ever said to me. They didn't think I could understand what they were talking about and when I tried to join in Auntie Nellie would say, "Little Pitchers have Big Ears!"

Anyway, that was how I got to know that Clem and Edna were both teachers. They'd been told to keep in touch with the daily news bulletins while they were on holiday, in case they were needed to help with evacuation of children. Barbara was with them, camping on a farm near Inverness *(there were no designated camp-sites – campers asked permission from farmers to camp on their land and the farmers provided them with water and milk)*, when they heard the news on their portable wireless that all teachers away on holiday must return home immediately. Clem's Mum, Auntie Nellie, had lots of money, so Clem had his own car *(not many people had cars in those days!)* and he'd driven all the way home through day and night along the Great North Road, so he must have been jolly worried!

Soon after Christmas the day came when I had to start school locally, having missed the first term of my first school year. Santa Claus had left me a little scooter – my most exciting Christmas present – so this made the journey to school a lot easier, because it was a long way to walk. As soon as I knew the right way, Mum let me go on my own, telling me not to talk to any strange men!

In the early days I was very impatient having to sit in a class that was learning the alphabet. Barbara had already taught me how to read at home in Vista Avenue, to stop me pestering everyone to 'Read me a story.' *Children learned how to read and spell phonetically, the same way as today's 'latest' method called 'synthetic phonics'.*

At home I'd already finished reading my favourite stories about Mumfie the Elephant; and at Auntie Nellie's house I worked my way through her big book of verses and pictures about the terrible things that happened to children who did wrong things – like Harriet who played with the matches, or Augustus who wouldn't eat his dinner. Both came to a dreadful end!

Out of school hours, I found the best way of escaping the grown-ups' attention was to go off exploring down the end of Auntie Nellie's long garden. It was quite easy to climb over the wooden bars of the fence, or wriggle beneath the lowest bar, and I discovered the world beyond was a farm. I could see two great shire horses plodding along in the distance. I daren't go in that direction in case someone told me off, so when I got tired of wandering about I made my way reluctantly back to the house to listen to the grown-ups talking.

Auntie Nellie got upset when there was talk of Clem being 'called up'. It was no good asking what *that* meant and anyway it didn't sound very interesting. When Dad was at home he usually kept quiet or just made jokes, but sometimes he got carried away and made a speech. I always knew when this was going to happen because he always began with "Now . . ." like the first one I could remember, when he started off, "Now, the day War broke out . . ." and Mum gave a deep sigh.

Bedtime for me was earlier than for anyone else, so it was not until I was a few months older (when we moved back to north London in the middle of the Blitz!) I discovered how serious grown-ups became when they were listening to the BBC 9-o'clock News, which told everyone how the war was going.

The so-called phoney war turned into real war for the soldiers of the BEF (British Expeditionary Force) in April 1940, when the Germans rapidly occupied Denmark and invaded Norway. The BEF was poorly equipped for fighting in Norway's snow-covered mountainous territory and was soon defeated by professional German alpine troops; but the Royal Navy won the battle against the German Navy and successfully extricated most of our soldiers who had managed to retreat to the coast.

The German Blitzkrieg (Lightning War) across Europe continued with the bombing, invasion and occupation of Holland, Belgium and Luxembourg.

(Sweden, Switzerland and Spain were the only European countries to remain neutral and unoccupied throughout the war – as did Eire.)

2. "We're On Our Own Now" ~ 1940

Now Dad was always talking about Dunkirk. What was Dunkirk?

May 1940. The fall of France. With the forced retreat of the British Expeditionary Force from Belgium into France, German troops swept across the frontier. To Churchill's despair (Winston Churchill had just replaced Chamberlain as Prime Minister) there were those in the French Government preparing to come to terms with the invaders. Paris was declared an 'open city' to save it from destruction. Under conflicting orders, the French army – at that time the biggest in Europe – fell back in disarray, along with the British, before the German onslaught. The survivors of the BEF, and those of the French troops who refused to surrender, became trapped on the beaches of Dunkirk as German forces reached Calais and glimpsed the white cliffs of Dover across the English Channel.

In the south of England, civilian boat-owners were called upon as a matter of urgency to help rescue our soldiers. About 600 little vessels gathered along the coast, forming an unlikely flotilla of fishing trawlers, river ferries, lifeboats, old holiday paddle-steamers and private launches, manned by older men or young boys who had not been called up to serve in the armed forces. These were led and escorted over the English Channel by ships of the Royal Navy.

Under enemy gunfire and falling bombs, both British and French soldiers, exhausted or wounded, were picked up from the beaches and ferried over to the big ships standing by or were taken in the little boats directly back to England. Many craft were damaged or sunk by mines or bombs, but the rest managed to save over 300,000 men (who abandoned or set fire to their equipment, guns, tanks, etc.) Those left behind were taken prisoner by the enemy.

I didn't take much notice when I heard Dad pronounce, "We're on our own now!" Dad was always making pronouncements – he was that sort of Dad. Then I heard someone on the wireless saying that Great Britain 'Stood Alone'. After that, there was much talk about 'Backs against the Wall!'

Another strange word I heard was 'Invasion'. This sounded a bit threatening, but I didn't really worry – the grown-ups could deal with *that*. That's what grown-ups were for…

I was shushed while the family listened to Churchill's speech on the wireless: "We shall Fight on the Beaches . . . we shall Fight in the Fields and in the Streets … we shall Fight in the Hills … we shall Never Surrender!" Well, thought I, of course we shall Never Surrender – nobody I knew would dream of doing such a thing!

In addition to the Home Guard (which consisted of older men or boys too young to be conscripted into the regular army), Churchill organized a secret army (unknown to the general public) of civilian volunteers, banded into small units across the southern counties and prepared, in the event of invasion, to gather intelligence and communicate by hidden radios. They were trained in guerrilla warfare, sabotage and killing silently with knives (BBC television documentary 2004).

To get out of Auntie Nellie's way, Dad took us out at the weekends for day-trips and picnics. Auntie Nellie was our weather forecaster. She looked out of the window and said, "Well, there's enough blue sky to make a sailor a pair of trousers, so it's going to be a fine day."

One Saturday we took a train to the seaside at Hastings, but I was terribly disappointed when I saw the beach barricaded with barbed wire. We set off for a walk on the grass above the cliffs and saw a group of people ahead, standing and staring out to sea. We came up to them on top of a little hill and discovered they were watching tiny planes far away, turning and diving over a convoy of ships outlined on the horizon. The sound of gunfire came across the water, then – a tiny burst of red and black against the blue. Somebody said, "He's going down!" Dad took us away, saying it was time for a bite to eat.

Hitler knew that any invasion fleet would be defeated by the Royal Navy. He wanted to destroy the Home Fleet, which defended the British Isles, but his Luftwaffe bombers were under constant attack by our fighter aircraft – Spitfires and Hurricanes. Hitler ordered Goering, Chief of the Luftwaffe, to eliminate RAF Fighter Command in preparation for the invasion and the Germans started bombing our airfields on the coast and around London.

It was a fine summer in 1940 and I looked forward to our day-trips by bus or coach to explore somewhere new and find a picnic spot. It was on one of these days out when I first saw the blue skies scribbled over with white, feathery trails, tracing the flights of Spitfires and enemy fighters chasing each other.

We sat on the grass, faces upturned, watching in silence while the 'dogfights' raged in silence across the sky – too high up to hear any sounds of battle. It all seemed strangely unreal. Here were the peaceful green fields and hedgerows slumbering in the warm sunshine, bees buzzing, while these white streaks and circles made lovely patterns against the blue summer skies. It looked more like an air display, put on for our entertainment, than a fight to the death.

Churchill called it the Battle of Britain. On the outcome depended our survival as a free nation.

Frank had a chart of the silhouettes of all the aircraft that had been designed up to that time. The Spitfire was easy to pick out – I already knew its distinctive shape – and Frank pointed out the Hurricane fighter and a bomber called the Wellington. He showed me the enemy planes – fighters called Messerschmitts, bombers called Heinkels, and a terrible dive-bomber known as the Stuka. Its engine screamed as it dived to bomb moving targets like ships or traffic.

The German planes outnumbered ours, at times by four to one, and our planes were being destroyed at a rate faster than replacements could be manufactured. Also, the number of deaths left a desperate shortage of experienced pilots and young RAF recruits were often sent into battle with only two or three weeks' training on fighter aircraft.

One advantage on our side was the British invention of radar in the late 1930s, which gave early warning of the approach of enemy aircraft. Young women recruited into the WAAF (Women's Auxiliary Air Force) worked at RAF stations to track, by radar, incoming enemy formations of planes in time for orders to be given to Spitfire pilots to 'Scramble!' and take off to intercept.

I heard Auntie Nellie talking to Mum and Dad about a German pilot who had crash-landed in a field and was found next morning by a group of small boys who took him home to one of their mothers. The mother called the police and while they were waiting she fried an egg with bacon for the German and made him a cup of tea. He was very polite and grateful before he was led off to become a POW (prisoner of war).

The family listened to Churchill speaking on the wireless: "Never, in the field of human conflict, was so Much owed, by so Many, to so Few." My Dad was much impressed by these words and quoted them for days afterwards – so I soon knew them off by heart.

By early September 1940, the RAF had won a significant victory. The Luftwaffe failed to gain control of the skies over southern England – the first conflict in several years in which the Germans met their match. If the young fighter pilots of the RAF had not prevailed, our island would have been invaded that autumn of 1940, changing the course of world history.

Also in September 1940, Hitler's invasion force – a flotilla of miscellaneous landing craft, amphibious tanks, tugs and transports lining the French coast – was revealed by photographic reconnaissance and became a target for RAF Bomber Command ('Invasion 1940' by Peter Fleming).

I could never tell whether Dad was serious or making jokes – he always kept a straight face – but I pricked up my ears when he talked about German spies dropping in by parachute, heavily disguised (he didn't say as what!), to get information from unsuspecting civilians going about their daily lives. From then on, I started looking at passers-by with new interest.

Dad also told us that all the signposts had been removed from crossroads and the names of railway stations blanked out, so the enemy wouldn't know where they were if they landed. *That* would make things difficult for them!

And for my benefit he quoted a verse addressed to Hitler:

> *Napoleon tried. The Dutch were on the way.*
> *A Norman did it – and a Dane or two.*
> *Some sailor-King may follow, one fine day.*
> *But not, I think, a low land-rat like you.*

I thought about this low land-rat with some scorn. Did he really think we would let him come and take over our country? At six years old, I got quite puffed up with indignation!

At Auntie Nellie's house we were all now sleeping downstairs on the floor in the hallway, Auntie Nellie in the cupboard under the stairs. I guessed the grown-ups were worried about bombs, but I knew they would get annoyed if I started asking questions.

It was a bit crowded with us all in the hallway. I never wanted to go to sleep and sometimes managed to put it off. "I'm hungry, please can I have a piece of toast?" This was always successful. It attracted Mum's attention, she couldn't tell me off for being hungry, I managed to delay going to sleep and the toast was an extra treat.

During the summer of 1940 the Germans had bombed airfields and aircraft production factories, some of them in areas around London, and bombs fell on a few scattered London suburbs ('Invasion 1940' by Peter Fleming); but the first of the big air-raids, on London's East End, docks and warehouses by the River Thames, started during the day on 7th September 1940 and continued through the night, leaving devastating damage and destruction over a large area.

The Germans only had to fly a short distance from airfields near the coasts of occupied countries. Our own bomber aircraft did not yet have a wide enough range to fly as far as Germany, make a serious attack and return, but on one occasion, in a symbolic gesture of retaliation for stray bombs on London, a small formation of Wellington bombers managed to get as far as Berlin to carry out a brief air raid. To do this they had to carry more fuel, fewer bombs. This attack on the capital of Germany enraged Hitler and he gave orders to the Luftwaffe to concentrate on London and bomb the civilian population into submission.

Evacuation of children, many of whom had returned home, took place a second time. It was around this time that 77 out of 90 children being evacuated to Canada lost their lives when the ship, City of Benares, taking them across the Atlantic, was struck by a German torpedo.

Clem had dug a big oblong pit in Auntie Nellie's garden for an air-raid shelter and Dad set about lining the walls of the pit with panels of corrugated iron and bolted them together. Then he bent the two sides over to meet at the top and bolted them together again to form the roof. *The Government organised deliveries of corrugated iron panels to those who had gardens.*

Everybody helped to pile earth over the steep curved roof and Dad cut out three or four deep steps in the ground leading down to the entrance. He covered the earth floor inside with duckboards and put up narrow wooden bunk-beds against the sides, leaving a walkway down the centre.

Auntie Nellie called it the Anderson shelter *(named after the government minister who thought of the idea)*, but Dad just called it the dug-out. As soon as it was ready, we started using the shelter as a family bedroom – all except for Aunty Nellie, who still crawled into the cupboard under the stairs every night. We had a small oil lamp – Dad called it the 'Hurricane' lamp – and a wireless *(on batteries)* and slept on pillows laid out on the bunk-beds. Instead of a door, there was a thick piece of material used as a curtain, which got muddier day by day.

I thought all this was glorious fun. Dad taught me how to play Cribbage – One for His Nob! We used Dad's old wooden cribbage board with matchsticks for pegs. Then Mum and Dad listened to the wireless, while Frank and I pretended to sleep. When I got into a drowsy state, the stale earthy smell inside the shelter made me dream of adventures in strange places.

One day I was scooting along as fast as I could to get home from school and spotted a metal tube lying in the roadway. We'd all been told not to touch strange metal objects lying on the ground in case they were unexploded shells from the ack-ack (anti-aircraft guns), so of course I was immediately attracted to this 'forbidden fruit'.

Anyway, it looked just like a plain tin tube with a lid. I picked it up nervously – careful not to open the lid, in case it went off Bang! – and carried it home, eager to show the grown-ups how brave I was. I was a bit taken aback when they immediately and fearlessly opened the lid. It turned out to be full of chocolate digestive biscuits – a rare luxury. The grown-ups thought it must have fallen off the back of an army truck. I heard them saying, "Patsy's very pleased with herself," and much to my delight, for the next few nights in the shelter, Mum doled out one chocolate biscuit each to Frank and me with our tin mugs of cocoa.

One night a huge explosion startled us all awake. Mum and Dad clambered out of the shelter to be confronted with the sight of Auntie Nellie crawling out of the back door in her nightie with rollers in her hair. She was calling out for her little terrier dog, Nipper. Both the front and back doors of the house had been blown open and the force of the blast had carried poor little Nipper straight through the house and up the length of the garden.

Clem came along to see us in the morning and there was much lively discussion as to whether the explosion was caused by a bomb or an anti-aircraft shell. Nipper was suffering so terribly with shock that Clem took him away to the vet – but he never came back. I thought Auntie Nellie must be very sad, but she never spoke about Nipper again.

Clem hadn't got his own Anderson shelter. He and Edna were sleeping in the cupboard under the stairs, the safest place in a house. For Barbara, Clem had removed some floorboards nearby and she crawled through as near as she could get to beneath the staircase. Barbara hated spending the nights like this. She said that lying on the ground she was shaken by the anti-aircraft guns, but what she complained about most was hearing mice scurrying nearby – and all this going on while she was studying for School Certificate!

Barbara followed the instructions put out on the wireless to keep a whistle, a bottle of water and a tin of biscuits with her, in case she was trapped under the rubble of a bombed house. *Although Cuffley was just beyond the edge of London, the bombers could be heard passing over and sometimes, on their way back, they got rid of any surplus bombs.*

Again we were woken up in the middle of the night. Clem, Edna and Barbara had all turned up very agitated. An air raid warden had banged on their front door and told them to get out of the house quickly, because a 'landmine' was hanging by its parachute from the branch of a tree outside one of the bedroom windows. Uncle Basil (Auntie Nellie's brother) and his wife arrived. They said that other people had also been turned out of their houses and they all had to go and wait in the parish hall until someone did something about the landmine.

The landmines were, in fact, naval magnetic mines powerful enough to sink our ships, but adapted by the enemy for dropping by parachute over built-up areas. They were timed to detonate a set period after landing, the purpose being to kill rescue workers or bomb disposal officers. When one exploded, it devastated an area half a mile around. At first, the only teams who knew how to defuse unexploded mines were those trained by the Royal Navy (BBC documentary 2005).

Clem said the Germans were returning to us the mines we had left behind after Dunkirk! It was several days before the bomb disposal squad arrived – they were in great demand – so Clem, Edna, Uncle Basil and his wife all had to spend the next few nights crowded together in Auntie Nellie's hall, with Aunty Nellie under the stairs and the rest of us in the Anderson shelter.

A few days later Barbara told us she'd heard a strange crackling noise in the morning as she walked down the hill from Enfield Chase station on her way to school. When she reached the town she saw shopkeepers sweeping up broken glass from the pavements – every shop window along the high street had been shattered by the blast from bombs.

3. "It's a Bomber's Moon Tonight!" ~ 1940

Dad and Frank went back to our old house one Saturday to see how the neighbours were getting on. By the time they reached Vista Avenue, a group of local boys were gathered out in the street watching German bombers flying very high overhead, on their way back home, with an escort of fighter planes – Messerschmitts – under attack from our Spitfires. One of the planes began a long dive with smoke streaming from its tail and everyone could see the parachute coming down when the pilot baled out. They all thought it was the enemy and cheered like mad. Then they all felt a bit silly because Dad pointed out that the plane was one of ours!

There was talk of moving back to Enfield, not just to be nearer Barbara's school but also because Frank had to go to his secondary school, which was, like Barbara's, on the safer side of Enfield – as safe as Cuffley, anyway. And Mum was desperate to have a home of her own again.

Returning to our old house seemed to be out of the question. It was not in a 'Safe Area' because there were munitions factories not far away in the valley of the River Lea – targets for enemy bombs. Nobody told me anything, but I still listened to the grown-ups' conversation!

Dad found a house to rent in a Safe Area. This was in Ridings Avenue, a small road ending a short distance away from a deep railway cutting and about 20 minutes walk from Enfield Town and the schools. The previous tenants had moved away soon after the war started – perhaps they didn't believe any part of London was safe! – so we were lucky to get such a beautiful house and garden in what my mother loved to call a Good Area. She was particularly proud that it was a detached house and I wondered briefly why detached houses were so special. It so happened that ours was the only fully detached house in the road; the others were all bigger, but semi-detached, so ours must have been built to use up a spare space.

My big sister came back to live with us. An Anderson shelter had already been dug in the garden, but Barbara announced that *she* was not going to sleep in it. "Hitler can do what he damn well likes, but I've had enough of going to bed in a hole in the ground on *his* account." After that, we all felt a bit cowardly about using the shelter and began life in our new home by going to bed upstairs in the normal way. I rather hoped the enemy was doing the same!

I was delighted to have the smallest bedroom – the 'box-room' – all to myself and even more delighted when I discovered that another little girl, Anne, lived a few houses away. Mum had to stop me calling round every day, asking her to come out to play. When she did come out we marked out the pavement with chalk to play hopscotch, or practised with our skipping ropes.

The first thing Mum wanted in our new house was a dog. She must have thought that what happened to Nipper in Cuffley was an unlikely one-off. Chum, our old black mongrel dog at Vista Avenue, had died before the war and Mum had always longed for a bull-mastiff, so very soon a golden female puppy arrived to live with us. Mum named her Juno and fed her on horsemeat, which was not on the ration *(by this time most kinds of meat were rationed)*. At first I had the idea that Juno would be my new playmate, but there was talk of school again, so I knew I would have to leave her behind.

I started at my new school, St. Andrew's Church Elementary School, on the far side (the town side) of Enfield Town Park, very late in the Autumn Term beginning my second year. Here it didn't take long to discover that I had to 'toe the line' or else!

First, there were morning prayers in the assembly hall; then we all trooped into the classroom and found our places. The teacher came in and we stood up and chorused, "Good Morning, Miss . . . . ." The pupils sat, two at each desk, in rows facing the teacher and blackboard, and everyone had to pay attention.

Our class teacher announced a gas-mask drill. Consternation! Everyone in the class was putting on a gas-mask. Did I ever have one? I couldn't remember. "Where is your gas-mask?" demanded the teacher, singling me out of the class. I stared at her, not knowing what to say. Tut tut! She produced a spare gas mask for me and I struggled to get it over my head like the other children. We had to keep the masks on for five minutes. I didn't much enjoy the experience. You had to make a conscious effort with breathing and there was a nasty smell of rubber. I wanted to protest about this, but the mask's protruding snout jumped up and down as I opened my mouth to speak and the eye-shield misted up with my breath.

Much to my dismay, I discovered that we always had to keep our gas masks with us wherever we were going. Everyone had a cardboard box with a string over the shoulder for carrying them around. Bother! I didn't want to be so encumbered. I'd only just started wearing a satchel and that was enough to hold my pencil box, skipping rope, the odd conker collected from the boys' conker games and so on. All the same, when I got home I demanded to know where my gas-mask was – why had Mum forgotten it? I didn't want to be singled out from the class again.

Instructions from the headmistress were: "If you hear the Air Raid Warning and you're less than half-way to school, you must run back home. If you're more than half-way, run on to the school as fast as you can." I lived rather further from school than most of the others and my idea was that the siren would only signal danger in Enfield Town – not in our Safe Area. I was quite pleased at the thought of having a morning off school.

By this time air-raid sirens had become a normal part of everyday life, wailing in the distance over central London or, quite often, much nearer in Enfield Town. The wailing noise always started deep down in the pit of my stomach, a split second before hitting my ears. It soared up to a crescendo, then sank down, over and over again for several minutes, before finally dying down to an uneasy silence. Then I listened, with a mixture of dread and excitement, for the first rumbling in the sky that meant enemy bombers approaching.

The first time Mum took me shopping in Church Street (the high street in Enfield Town) the siren went off, but no-one appeared to show much alarm – they just started walking a bit faster! A policeman tried to hurry people along to a shelter, but Mum and I just wanted to get home and the bombers must have passed by while we were crossing the park.

An air raid meant shrapnel from the anti-aircraft guns falling in the streets. The boys at school were turning up with collections of shrapnel and we all joined in a fierce competition, bragging to each other about having the biggest single piece or the largest collection.

On a morning when the siren went off as I was a bit more than half-way to school, I hurried on and found my classmates outside the school gate, crouching down around glowing red pieces of shrapnel, waiting for them to cool off, but the teacher came out and spoilt everything by chivvying everyone into the school shelter.

If there was an Air Raid Warning during school time, everybody had to troop into the shelter underneath the playground and sit on long benches against the cold concrete walls. Here the teachers made us pass the time by chanting times-tables, but as it was so dark inside the shelter we managed to whisper and giggle together without attracting their attention. They wouldn't let us out until the All Clear, when we had to go back to lessons.

Our teachers were very stern about behaviour in class. Anyone who stepped out of line got a severe ticking off or was even sent out to stand in the corridor outside the classroom.

I was learning fast that certain things were Not Done. One of the things that was Not Done was to kick up a fuss. "Pull yourself together!" That was from the teachers. "You mustn't tell tales about anyone!" *That* was from my classmates. My Auntie Nellie had already done *her* share by telling me that I must respect my Elders and Betters and consider others before myself. *(Such terms as 'politically correct' or, for example, 'racism' were not yet in our language. Good Manners were expected to cover everything!)*

The boys ran around with arms outstretched pretending to be fighter planes. They made up gangs to rival each other in making mischief. One of the gangs included a black boy – the only black child in the school and the first one I'd ever seen. He was rather shy and not as boisterous as the others; he was the only one who didn't shout insults at the girls! *(I never saw any bullying and no-one had heard of social workers, but for older boys at secondary school there was the threat of being sent to an Approved School, or Borstal, for any violent or criminal behaviour.)*

Not to be outdone, the girls also formed gangs and I was delighted when I was invited to join a gang led by a lively little girl called Shirley – now I'd been accepted!

We little girls all boasted to each other about our mothers: "*My* mother is the Best Mother in the World." Trying to score a point, I boasted that *my* mother had a Real Gold Bedspread. They all scoffed at me and when I stopped to think it dawned upon me that it was actually just shiny golden satin. I was properly deflated!

Once we were all in the playground when a solitary plane flew very fast overhead. There had been no air raid warning but the boys all shouted in excitement because they recognised it as an enemy plane – it had black crosses on the wings. On our own planes there was a friendly circle filled in with red, white and blue.

Huge grey barrage balloons floated in the sky over London. They were enormous – bigger than houses. Each had two fins like big ears sticking out at one end. In the sunshine I thought they looked beautiful, bright silver with their sides rippling in the breeze. At first I was puzzled as to what use they could be against bombs, but then found out they were to protect road traffic against dive-bombers, or to prevent low-flying aircraft from machine-gunning civilians in the streets. *In France the Germans had flown their planes, a few feet above ground, machine-gunning streams of refugees escaping from the invading troops.*

At night there was the Blackout. Showing any light anywhere in the country was strictly forbidden, so every window had to be covered with blackout curtains. The lamp-posts stayed unlit and the traffic crawled along with dimmed and shaded headlights. Imagine the great city of London at night – all black without a single chink of light! People were constantly bumping into lamp-posts or each other. They carried shaded torches, which had to be kept pointed downwards, to see where they were going.

On a clear night, the big, brilliant stars scattered across the dark sky were a beautiful sight – no lights down here to get in the way and dim their sparkle. The Milky Way arched over the world like a ghostly bridge.

The Germans had settled down to regular night-time bombing. If the moon was full, or near to full, the word went round: "It's a Bomber's Moon tonight!" What use was Blackout when the enemy pilots could see the glint of the River Thames leading them to a city they could see clearly in bright moonlight?

Dad swore that Mum could hear the enemy planes taking off, because she always sat up in bed and said, "Hark!" at least five minutes before the siren sounded. To make a better joke of it, Dad said she could hear them take off from Berlin. It was some time before I realised they only had to fly from airfields in France, Belgium or Holland.

Following Mum's "Hark!" we all rushed out of our rooms carrying our pillows, bumping into each other on the landing, to go downstairs to the shelter. It took a few minutes to get there. We had to go down two steep concrete steps outside the back door, run round the corner of the house, then down several steps past the coal-shed to reach the grass and finally clamber down the slippery earth steps into the shelter. I usually arrived breathless, enjoying the feel of the cold, damp grass under the soles of my bare feet and getting told off by Mum for forgetting my slippers – as though *that* mattered, I thought crossly.

One night, sirens wailing, Mum came running out of the bedroom carrying three or four pillows and couldn't stop herself from falling down the stairs. The pillows saved her. She was bouncing on them by the time she reached the bottom and she got right up and carried on running, through the house and back door (back doors were never locked – it saved time) and down all the way to the shelter, with my brother and me on her heels. Mum swore afterwards that she hadn't even noticed – and this story was told, and embellished with each telling, to entertain visitors for the rest of the war.

Inside the shelter nobody spoke while bombers were droning overhead. Somehow they seemed more threatening in the darkness – engines throbbing, heavy and out of sync, loaded down with the bombs they carried. They sounded quite different from our Spitfires, which roared across the sky, a few at a time.

I listened fearfully to the big anti-aircraft guns banging away in the park, shaking the ground. Sometimes a bomb exploded too near for comfort, but with all the noise of the guns it was hard to tell in which direction. When the bombers had passed over we felt safe again, listening to gunfire and explosions further away over central London. Sometimes the air raids went on all night. *Waves of bombers came over at intervals while others were leaving.*

Peeping out of the shelter I saw the long beams of the searchlights, like white pencils moving over the black sky. Once I saw a tiny plane far up get caught in two searchlight beams as they crossed over each other. Then the other beams moved over until they were all covering the plane in white light, making it a clear target. I had a momentary inkling of sympathy, but then – why did they fly over to drop bombs on us?

In the early morning, the siren sounded the All Clear – a steady high note of satisfaction, meaning the skies were clear of enemy bombers and Mum could make a cup of tea. When I set off for school I watched out for pieces of shrapnel to add to my collection.

Dad to Mum at various breakfast times:

"The East End's had a terrible pasting."

"Landmine down in Holborn."

"The City's burning. It's the Great Fire of London all over again."

"It's a miracle – St. Paul's still standing."

"Now the West End has had a taste of it."

"Cheeky blighter! Scored a hit on Buckingham Palace."

I heard Dad telling Mum that the Eastenders distrusted the brick public shelters erected by the Government and crowds were flocking to the underground tube stations every night, bringing improvised beds to spread out on the platforms. When they first started doing this, they had to buy penny tickets to go down the escalators. Dad said the Government had made several unsuccessful attempts to stop this flagrant disregard for authority, but finally had to give in. The WRVS (Women's Royal Voluntary Service) took charge and came along with trolleys of tea, to keep order and hand out refreshments.

As the Blitz wore on, entertainers came down to the underground shelters and played music, cracked jokes or started a sing-song with the shelterers.

One morning Dad arrived at work to find heaps of smoking rubble where his office used to be. After a lot of time spent coming to and fro and meeting various people, he got very busy organising the front room as an office and furnished it with a big dark green steel desk and three dark green steel cupboards the size of wardrobes. Mum was jolly pleased to have Dad at home all day and now we had the luxury of a telephone.

It was then I found out that my Dad worked as General Secretary of a small trade union, the National Union of Scalemakers. At the age of 17 he had signed up to fight in the Great War *(the First World War)* and his experiences in the battlefield trenches, where he got to know his fellow soldiers, had left him resolved to do what he could to improve the lot of 'the working man' and to take part in the development of the Trade Unions. His main interest, as I later understood it, was to get justice or compensation for men who had suffered industrial accidents or injury.

Like most people, Dad called the enemy 'Jerry' but sometimes he used the word 'Hun', which sounded even more sinister, and Mum would tell him to stop being so old-fashioned! I understood then that our soldiers had called the enemy 'the Hun' in the Great War. Dad had survived the terrible battle of Passchendaele, but one of his fingers had been shot off. This happened just as he was lifting a mug of tea to his lips – the soldier sitting next to him was killed by the bullet, so my Dad had a lucky escape.

Dad had a painting on the wall of his office – a picture of a farmhouse in a bleak, empty landscape. He told me it was where he and his gunner crew had sheltered in a barn for a night or two between the battles *(at Ypres)* and one of his mates had painted it.

(When my Dad was in his 80th year, my brother Frank took him to visit, for the first time since the First World War, the Flanders battlefields. They found the farm where Dad's mate painted his picture and – still living there – the actual descendants of the people who gave them shelter in their barn. Dad was overwhelmed when they gave him a great welcome. "You must come in and have champagne ... we owe you gratitude ... we shall never forget!")

We all had to shout when we spoke to Dad, because he'd been deafened by the big guns. The story was that he'd fallen asleep, lying by a gun carriage, when a battle started and the gunner crew, out of devilment, left him asleep when they fired off the gun. They must have thought it a great joke when he woke up in fearful alarm, but my Dad's eardrums were permanently blasted. Although he wore a hearing aid, he was always fiddling with it to get it adjusted properly and we always had to shout at him. Poor old Dad ...

In spite of his deafness, the neighbours asked my Dad to be the Air-Raid Warden for our road and he kept buckets of water, stirrup pumps and sandbags in the driveway ready to deal with incendiaries. Later, I found out that incendiary bombs were dropped first to start fires, so that the German pilots could see where to drop their 'High Explosives' or 'Aitch Eees', a term often used with some relish by Dad.

From time to time the sirens remained silent and the night passed without interruptions. There were reports on the wireless of air raids on other cities across Britain, but on the odd occasion Londoners could take a breather.

At intervals during the sustained Blitz on London, attacks were also carried out on industrial cities and ports vital to our economy and military capability. In one air raid on Coventry, an important engineering centre, thousands of incendiaries were dropped, prior to heavy bombing with high explosives. All the heart of the city, along with its loved, beautiful, 14th century cathedral, was totally destroyed and hundreds of lives lost. After the first shock, despair and grief, the spirit of the people of Coventry turned to defiance and determination. They brought the armaments factories back to production again within a few weeks.

This terrible attack on Coventry was one of those which led Bomber Harris to declare: "THEY have sown the Wind and THEY will reap the Whirlwind."

---

4. The 2ⁿᵈ Great Fire of London ~ 1940/41

In the Christmas holidays, Mum and Dad took me to go shopping at Gamages, a famous store in Holborn, where I set my heart on a beautiful rocking-horse, almost half life-size, with leather saddle and bridle, costing £5.5s.0d. But Mum said it was out of the question – five 'guineas' was a fortune. To cheer me up, Dad took us for tea at Lyons Corner House at Marble Arch. The band played in the tea-room and I was allowed to have a very expensive Knicker-Bocker Glory for one shilling and sixpence *(18 old pence)*, a rare treat.

Mum always made Christmas magical. A few weeks earlier, she made the Christmas Pudding, stirring in five thru'penny bits *(3d each or three old pence)* one for each of the family. My job was to brush these clean in soapy water beforehand. After the mixing-bowl had been emptied, Mum gave me a spoon to scrape out and eat the last bits of delicious raw mixture.

A week before Christmas Day, Dad went down to Enfield Town Market and brought home a Christmas Tree, which I 'helped' to decorate. Frank and I made coloured paper chains for Dad to hang across the ceiling. We also collected holly branches with bright red berries from along the lane through the golf-links.

In the Christmas holidays I was always taken to a matinee performance of the Pantomime – that year it was 'Cinderella' – and there were other treats at this time: sometimes a visit to Selfridges to see Santa Claus, or to Hamleys, the famous toy-shop, where the shop assistants demonstrated an enormous model railway, the layout spread out all over the floor. But anything I wanted always cost too much!

I had to get presents for everyone with my pocket money, helped out with a bit extra from Mum. My Christmas Shopping, which was of great importance to *me*, seemed to be a bit of a joke for the family. I was very cross when I overheard Mum and Frank having a good laugh at my expense. Mum was telling Frank that I had already got his present, it was in a tube and had something to do with his teeth!

Anyway, I found the perfect thing for Mum – a brooch of letters stating plainly, "*MOTHER*" in mother-of-pearl, price 6d *(six old pence)* in Woolworths. I bought it, thinking how delighted she would be, but was later disappointed to find that she was reluctant to wear it when she went out. I simply couldn't understand why!

On Christmas Eve Mum spent the afternoon plucking a big bird, filling the kitchen with floating feathers. I darted about full of excitement, with everybody telling me to get out of their way. On the wireless Bing Crosby was crooning a new song, 'I'm Dreaming of a White Christmas', making everything even more exciting.

As we could never be sure whether there would be an air raid warning loud enough for our area to send us to the shelter in the middle of the night, I hung my stocking on the door-handle of the sitting room to make it easier for Santa Claus. Despite growing suspicions – I couldn't see how anybody could squeeze down our narrow sooty chimney – I wasn't going to be done out of the traditional stocking.

That night, however, there were no air raids at all over any part of London. In the morning I found my stocking duly filled with little gifts – a bubble-blower shaped like a man's smoking pipe, a 'magic' slate, a kaleidoscope, a box of crayons and so on, with a tangerine and a silver sixpence in the toe. Tangerines never appeared at other times – they were part of the Christmas magic. *(I didn't know then, but that was my last tangerine for years to come!)*

For me the most exciting part of the day was immediately after breakfast, when we all sat round the blazing fire – Dad always made sure we had enough coal for a good fire at Christmas – with mysterious, brightly coloured packages lying under the Christmas Tree in the corner; and started unwrapping everybody's presents.

Usually there were new books for me, my favourite kind of present, often by Enid Blyton, but sometimes one of the classics, such as 'Alice in Wonderland'; 'Winnie the Pooh'; 'The Wind in the Willows'; 'Peter Pan'; or 'The Water Babies'. *(All I can remember from 'The Water Babies' is the character called Mrs Do-as-You-Would-Be-Done-By!)*

There were no 'abridged' versions for children and most of the books available in the shops were in 'utility' wartime bindings. Paperbacks appeared later in the 1950s.

Christmas Day passed, eating too much, laughing too much, staying up late and playing games and charades. Jerry very kindly stopped bombing for a couple of nights. I thought he must want to enjoy his Christmas too.

A few nights after Christmas I half woke up, my nose twitching. There was something in the air – like the smell of fireworks on Guy Fawkes' Night. Still half asleep, I lay there remembering the last Bonfire Night we'd celebrated before the war when Frank tied a Catherine Wheel on the fence and Dad lit a sparkler for me to hold. Then, suddenly wide-awake, I found myself alone in the shelter with the rumbling noise, like heavy thunder, of continuous bombing.

I got up hurriedly, climbed out to look for the others and got a terrible shock. Night had turned into day – with an orange-coloured sky! I ran up the steps and round the corner of the house and saw the houses on the opposite side of the road, clearly lit up beneath the bright orange glow. I knew Dad must be on watch somewhere and perhaps Barbara was at a friend's house, but where were Mum and Frank? Perhaps Frank too was at a friend's house. In that case, *where was Mum?*

There was no let-up from the noise of bombing. It sounded as though Jerry was in a very bad temper! I clambered up the back-door steps and hurried through the house, peeping into each empty dark room downstairs and getting more and more alarmed. Then in a panic I ran upstairs. I spied Dad wearing his 'tin hat' and standing on the little balcony outside Frank's bedroom in the front of the house – and panic turned to joy and relief.

In his role as an air-raid warden, Dad had got a couple of steel helmets and some black armbands with large white letters sewn on them – ARP – standing for Air Raid Precautions. Still in my pyjamas and before Dad could catch sight of me, I ran off to find the spare tin hat and an arm-band. Putting these on made me feel extremely brave and important and I hurried back to take my place next to Dad as, I thought proudly, 'Assistant Air Raid Warden'.

We lived at the top of a hill and from the front of the house looked south, where the sky was angry red over central London, lightening to an unearthly bright orange above our heads and illuminating the whole street. I was entranced – it was such a strange and beautiful sight. It was even stranger, in the middle of that freezing cold winter's night, to feel gusts of warm wind on my cheeks. Along with the smell of fireworks, I spotted tiny black smuts drifting in the air. Looking more closely I saw they were burnt bits of paper.

It was all so exciting I wanted to talk to Dad about it but when I looked up and saw his face I changed my mind. Normally, he would say, "Hello, Scallywag!" whenever I came along, but this time he didn't even seem to notice I was there. I stood next to him, taking care to keep very still. I wondered if he was thinking about the Other War. I wondered if he was very angry with the Germans.

I thought I'd better not say anything or I might get sent back to bed in the shelter. We both just stood there, side by side in the beautiful orange light, listening to the deep rolling thunder of the bombs and staring at the flickering red glow in the south. Perhaps Dad was thinking about the poor people in the middle of it all. Then a new thought struck me – would there be anything left of London in the morning?

I knew how much my Dad loved London. He took great delight in telling everyone he was a true Cockney, born within the sound of Bow Bells. *(He had actually been born in the City, but he came from an educated family so he didn't have a Cockney accent. It was my mother who was a true East Ender.)* Dad was always telling me things about London, so I learned a lot from him, and in the first few weeks of the air raids, he was always talking about the East End and the Docks, which Jerry was bent on destroying.

Dad told me that before the War the great Port of London was filled with hundreds of merchant ships from every nation, crowding the River Thames from Tilbury all the way to the Tower of London. Lining the banks of the great river, downstream from Tower Bridge, there were bonded warehouses filled with brandy or oriental carpets, and others filled with grain, oil, rubber, timber, molasses, sugar and so on. London was a big manufacturing city, quite apart from the industrial cities of the North. It was also the most important financial centre in the world. *Lloyds is still the biggest marine insurance business in the world today, covering most international shipping.*

Mum eventually turned up on that fearful night and I was so pleased to see her I never thought to ask where she had been. In any case, I was hoping she wouldn't take it into her head to tell me to go back to bed. There was not long to go until morning and the bombing was becoming more sporadic. When she made a cup of tea for Dad and herself and a piece of toast and cocoa for me, I took it as my reward for being an Assistant Air Raid Warden.

> *The night of 29th December 1940, when the whole of the City of London was in flames, was one of the worst raids of the Blitz, known as the Second Great Fire of London, the greatest fire in recorded history up to that time. A dramatic blow-by-blow account of that night is given in the book 'Blitz' by M.J. Gaskin.*

On the way to visit a family in Enfield, Mum led me past a row of houses where a bomb had blasted away the front halves of all of them. It was a strange feeling looking into the inside of other people's private homes. The wallpaper had torn edges where the wall was ripped away. I could see a bath with great cast iron feet standing crazily on half a floor upstairs in one house and a staircase that started half-way up in another. There were beds fallen through ceilings and a piano still standing but covered with rubble and plaster dust.

Poor Juno! One weekend the blast from an explosion blew open the front door, Juno bolted outside and my brother Frank bolted after her. He managed to grab hold of her, but she was so terrified she gave him a savage bite on the hand. Mum was broken-hearted, but Dad was quite firm about it; the kindest thing she could do for Juno was to take her to the vet to be put to sleep, for who could tell how long the air raids would go on? The next time I got home from school I found Juno missing and wondered sadly how many other beloved pets were meeting the same fate.

One day Barbara came back from school jolly pleased with life. She told me that Hitler had bombed the school gym during last night's air-raid. If there was one thing Barbara hated at school, it was gym. The girls had to run across the playing fields dressed only in their gym kit, even in the freezing winter, to get to the gymnasium, which was in a separate, unheated building. Now the building had been "destroyed by a direct hit – hooray!"

Then one evening Barbara arrived home very late. She'd gone to see a friend in Enfield and was already on her way back in the dark when the siren went off. She thought there was enough time to get home before the air raid got under way, but the bombers came overhead, the ack-ack (anti-aircraft gunfire) started up and a lot of red-hot shrapnel began to fall in the street.

When a big glowing piece of shrapnel whistled down just a hairsbreadth past Barbara's nose and dropped with a clang at her feet, she got a bad shock. Just then she heard the whistling sound of a falling bomb and dashed through the nearest front gate. She fell against the door of the house, which immediately opened, and a man's hand came out. He grabbed her arm, pulled her inside – no time for a word! – and they both dived under a table as the house shook with the blast. They stayed there while the enemy aircraft were droning overhead until the noise of gunfire and bombing died down. Then Barbara's host whispered, "I'll just take a look outside and see if they've passed over," and Barbara decided to hurry on home.

Bomb damage was quite extensive in the Enfield borough. The Germans targeted the Small Rifles Factory, which manufactured guns called Lee Enfield, and several other armaments factories in the Lea Valley.

Now aged 16, Barbara volunteered for fire-watching duty once a week at St. Andrew's Church at the back of the market square in Enfield Town. I was rather jealous of this – grown-ups got all the interesting things to do! It never occurred to me to wonder how Barbara would save the church if it caught fire. As far as I was concerned my big sister could cope with everything, so I was hardly worried.

Dad told me later that fire-watchers in the centre of London stood on the roof-tops of big buildings during an air raid, watching out for falling incendiaries. They smothered as many of these as they could with sandbags to prevent fires from spreading. All civilians between ages 16 and 60 were expected to take turns at this duty. And there were quite a few boys younger than 16 who were enthusiastic volunteers. It was more of a thrill than going to bed for the night.

In St Andrew's Church, Barbara and her friend Susan, who lived across the road and had volunteered to go with her, slept on the long, narrow pew cushions in the tower under the clock, which clanked every quarter of an hour – so not much sleep! They were equipped with buckets of water, buckets of sand and stirrup pumps.

Once an H.E. (high explosive) fell on the church but, luckily for Barbara and Susan, not on a night they were there.

Often I heard Dad talk about UXBs. I didn't ask what these were. There were so many strange combinations of letters used at that time and, as far as I was concerned, it was just another of the grown-ups' codes used to prevent me from knowing their secrets.

UXBs – unexploded bombs – caused much loss of life. Some were bombs that failed to detonate but most were deliberately time-delayed to kill any rescue workers. They had to be defused before they could be removed, which was a delicate and dangerous procedure. No sooner had the intricacies of one type of fuse been resolved and dealt with, then another kind was discovered, often with an extra booby trap, for the enemy was continually coming up with all sorts of cunning devices. Bomb disposal squads worked under the threat of being blown up at any moment.

As time went on I found out what UXBs were. It was during a family conversation about Conscientious Objectors – young men who refused to be conscripted to fight in the military services because it was against their principles to kill other human beings. Mum was inclined to suspect they were cowards, pretending to have these principles as an excuse not to fight, but Dad told her that quite a few of them were risking their lives by working in the unexploded bomb disposal squads, so they couldn't *all* be cowards. He also said that in any case it was a good thing we had a Parliamentary system which allowed the choice of being a Conscientious Objector.

5. "London Can Take It" ~ 1941

On BBC television, long after the war was over, a woman was questioned about her experiences in London during the Blitz. "But we didn't have all the worries that people have today. There were only two things to think about – where to sleep the next night and what to eat for the next meal. That concentrated the mind wonderfully!"

On our occasional trips to the West End we usually went by trolley-bus from Enfield Town to Tottenham Court Road, where we had to get off and walk. We passed by half-broken buildings with huge gaps between them. Sometimes just one wall was left standing. In central London the big buildings had piles of sandbags against the outside walls. In Oxford Street there were rubble-filled spaces between the stores. The surviving stores had notices in front, 'Open as Usual'; or even – with their frontage windows blasted away – 'We are More Open than Usual!'

We visited Auntie Louie, who lived in a flat along the Charing Cross Road. Going along the London streets, I spotted a lot of signboards with a big white letter S (for Shelter) and a white arrow to show the way. Mum told me that the big buildings offered shelter in their basements or cellars to any passers-by during air-raids, but some people said they became death traps if there was a direct hit. I heard there was a good deal of joking and singing in the shelters to keep spirits up. The noisier the raid, the louder the singing!

Everyone was saying, "London can Take It!" But my Mum said, "How much longer will London have to Take It?"

Our neighbours along the road were always dropping in for a cup of tea and a chat. I listened avidly to the conversation going on and picked up a lot of information. If people were bombed out of their homes, they were taken in by their neighbours. If whole streets had been bombed to rubble, the Government arranged for school buildings to be opened to shelter survivors for a night or two, until their friends or relatives could make arrangements to accommodate them. The WRVS brought blankets, made tea, comforted people and joked with them to keep up their spirits.

I knew about the official services such as the Fire Brigade, Ambulance Service and Police, but Dad said the first on the scene were usually the fire-watchers or the Air Raid Wardens *(all unpaid volunteers)*, who co-ordinated help from everyone around to dig people, dead or alive, out of the rubble. Women helped by driving ambulances, while others brought blankets or made tea.

Young women were 'called up' with the choice of either joining one of the military services or taking over the jobs left behind by the men who had been called up. *Some women in the ATS (the women's army called the Auxiliary Territorial Service) worked on barrage balloon sites and with the anti-aircraft gun crews.*

Bus drivers were all men, but many of the conductors were women, known as 'clippies'. They wore the heavy ticket-clipping machines on a leather strap over their shoulders. Some young women were Land Girls, employed as farm labourers, milking cows, driving horse-drawn or motorised tractors and bringing in the harvest; and women also took jobs on the railways as guards, or in signal-boxes, pulling the heavy levers to change the points along the track, while others cleaned and oiled the locomotives.

Sometimes Mum took me on the train to Kings Cross. We used the branch line of the LNER – London & North-Eastern Railway –and then caught a bus to Oxford Street.

LNER was one of four companies which owned the railway system. Each company controlled its own geographical area with its own track, locomotives and carriages. Unlike today's preserved steam trains, where speed is restricted, the old steam trains were generally as fast as today. A long-distance, non-stop express could reach speeds of 100 mph or more. In the 1930s Great Britain held the record for the fastest steam train, the Mallard, at 126 mph, still valid today.

Before the war, trains arrived dead on time. Only thick fog made the occasional exception. There were no disruptions caused by 'leaves on the line' because the weight of the locomotives, over 100 tons, kept the wheels on the track at any speed, no matter how wet and slippery the fallen leaves.

A safety measure used then was called ATC – Automatic Train Control – whereby a raised ramp, fitted between the rails ahead of a signal, lifted a 'shoe' on the train to apply the brakes for a red signal. This action could be cancelled by an electric charge if the signal was green.

Before the war started, Mum and Dad had taken Frank and me on the Great Western Railway. It was a long train journey to stay for a holiday with Uncle Jack (really our 'Great Uncle' because he had married my Dad's Aunt Phoebe) who lived by the sea in Brixham, Devon. The London main-line station was filled with hurrying passengers. A coal fire blazed in the waiting room. Porters were carrying luggage and finding seats for passengers. "Back or Facing, Madam?"

Setting off was quite a ceremony. The Station Master stood by, looking very grand in his brass-buttoned uniform and peaked cap. On the platform the guard, also in uniform, took his watch from his waistcoat pocket to check the time, while the big station clock ticked away the minutes to departure. The train driver leaned out of his cab, looking back at the guard, waiting for his signal. Then – a shrill blast on the guard's whistle, a wave of his green flag, and the train started off with a WHOOSH of escaping steam. We were off! As the train left the outskirts of London, the wheels on the track settled down into a fast rhythmic beat, just right for chanting – dadadi-*dah*, dadadi-*dah*!

Starting out on another journey, I saw a latecomer dash on to the platform, waving his ticket at the man at the barrier, and race alongside the train as it moved off, relying on some obliging soul to hold the door open for him until he could leap into the carriage before the train picked up speed. *(I did the same thing later in life and was helped in the same way, for all the old trains had slam doors – as well as windows which could be opened. It was taken for granted that people took responsibility for their own safety.)*

My Dad told me that on the railway it was 'up' to London and 'down' to everywhere else in the country. He said that you could always tell which way you were going by looking at the tall, wooden telegraph poles which ran alongside the track. The crosspieces were fixed on the side towards London.

Once, with Mum and Dad on Victoria station to meet somebody *(it must have been before the war)*, I'd seen the Boat Train, the Golden Arrow, waiting by the platform, with the tables inside covered in white tablecloths and lighted red lamps. I envied the people boarding, with their heavy trunks handled by the porters, off to the exciting unknown world abroad. Dad told me later that you could buy a ticket to cover a journey across Europe, travelling by boat train and cross-channel ferry, all arranged by the man in the local ticket office. Dad also told me that when he was a young man you could even get a ticket from Charing Cross straight through to Moscow!

Now in wartime everything was different. The trains were often late or filled with troops. Most of the porters had disappeared, called up to serve in the armed forces. Waiting with Mum on Enfield Chase station for the train to Kings Cross, I saw a large poster with the words, 'Is Your Journey Really Necessary?' I saw these posters on every station whenever we travelled by train.

Railway workers had to repair bomb damage on London's extensive railway network, while the Fire Brigade struggled every night to save buildings in flames and the Heavy Rescue and Salvage services worked to clear the streets of rubble, dig for those who were buried underneath and repair broken gas and water mains.

I heard a lot about 'Doing your Bit'. Everyone was expected to be a Good Neighbour because we were 'all in the same boat' and total strangers offered friendship and hospitality to anyone in need who came their way. Our own neighbours talked about picking their way over rubble every morning on the way to work. If their places of work were still standing, they often found the windows blasted out of existence.

Everybody seemed quite matter-of-fact about it. There was no question of letting it interfere with daily routine. I heard about office staff working in rooms half-filled with rubble and someone saw a typist rattling away at a desk on the pavement outside broken walls. Bus services ran as normal but during an air-raid the driver stopped the bus whenever someone hailed him, just as though he were a taxi-driver. Nobody had to find a bus stop – people just waved at the driver.

In the city centre the bus-driver often had to choose his route to avoid bomb-cratered roads. When an air raid was at its height, a bus sometimes came looming out of the smoke to pick up people wanting to get out of the area.

Milkmen still delivered every morning, leaving bottles standing on the doorsteps of any offices or dwellings left standing amid the smashed buildings.

When Post Offices were bombed out, the staff set up temporary post offices in various odd places. Postmen sometimes had to dig away at the rubble to uncover pillar boxes and collect the mail. As telephone lines were often broken, messengers on bicycles pedalled furiously along streets dodging bomb craters and heaps of rubble.

Outside the shops and market-stalls in Enfield Town there were notices saying things like, 'Never Mind Hitler – Business as Usual' or 'We're Still Open for Our Customers.' And I spotted a lot of posters about the streets, stuck on walls everywhere: 'Dig for Victory'; 'Careless Talk Costs Lives'; 'Watch Out – the Squanderbug's About'; 'Make Do and Mend'; and so on.

The posters had colourful pictures, which were something to look at when I had to go on boring shopping trips with Mum. I liked especially the one with a country scene of patchwork fields and hedges and a farm worker following a pair of shire horses drawing a plough over the brow of a hill. It had the words, 'This is *YOUR* Country. *FIGHT* for It!'

The horse was my favourite animal. Every morning the milkman's horse, Bob, came clopping along the road pulling the milkcart. When I heard him coming to a stop outside our house, I hurried out to stroke his nose and give him a piece of apple or carrot. Bob was huge, gentle and patient with beautiful brown eyes and long black eyelashes and I loved him.

Getting up in time for school, running upstairs to get dressed and down again for breakfast, satchel bumping, wishing I could stay at home with the sound of cheerful brass bands on the wireless, Mum bustling around, lighting the coal fire for Dad in his office and stoking up the coke boiler fire in the kitchen. Sometimes I even wished the Air Raid Warning would go off again so that I could stay at home, but now it never wailed in the mornings. Out into the cold on my scooter, scarf wrapped round nose and ears.

I caught the measles and was put to bed in the front room, which Dad used as his office. Dr Adams said I had to stay in a darkened room, so Dad put the three tall steel cupboards across the middle of his office and worked on one side of them by the windows, while Mum made up a bed for me on the 'dark' side of the room. I was very interested in my big red spots and lay in bed peering into a hand-mirror and counting them on my face. Mum popped in and out with drinks and I felt very special.

For some time Frank had been filling his quota of Good Deeds as a Boy Scout by going round to old people's houses to help them bolt together the new indoor shelters *(invented by Herbert Morrison, a Labour member of Churchill's coalition Government)*.

As Mum didn't want to take me down to the dug-out when I had a temperature, Dad had arranged for a Morrison shelter to be delivered. With Frank giving a hand, he set it up against the back of the heavy metal cupboards which divided 'office' from 'bedroom'. It was made of steel, table-height, just a low cage with a thick solid roof, and the area inside was about the size of a long double bed. We all had to sleep across it in a row with our legs sticking out on one side. Dad, nagged by Mum in one of her house-proud moments, painted it dark green to match his green steel office furniture.

Now, instead of going upstairs to bed and rushing down again when the local siren went off, we slept all night and every night in the Morrison shelter. Dad was fond of making dire predictions about the whole family ending up without any legs by the end of the war, but we were all used to his dire predictions and took no notice. After all, we did live in a Safe Area. Even so, I made sure my feet were tucked up well away from the edge of the cage. It was easier for me as I was the smallest. Sometimes, when I had one of my infections, I slept underneath Dad's big steel desk.

That year I was away from school more often than at it! After the measles, I had chicken pox, German measles *(rubella)* and whooping cough. The family got very worried when I was whooping most of the night, but it didn't really hurt and I enjoyed all the sympathy and attention. It was an anti-climax when I got better and had to go back to school.

The 'common-sense' view prevailing at the time was that childhood infections were nature's way of building up a healthy immune system for protection in later life, when the same infections would be more serious. Antibiotics were not yet in general use, but there were vaccinations for some dangerous diseases such as smallpox and diphtheria (and hospitals were spotlessly clean with Matron to supervise the nurses and the Almoner to deal with social problems).

From grown-ups I was always hearing the old sayings such as 'an apple a day keeps the doctor away', meaning that you should eat plenty of fruit and vegetables to keep healthy. And on an occasion when my knee turned septic after a fall, Mum used the traditional remedy of wrapping my knee in a hot bread poultice to draw out the poison.

As Jerry bombed only at night-time, it was safe going to the cinema in the afternoons. On Saturdays, or in the school holidays, Mum took me to see the new Walt Disney films in colour – a new one was launched every year: 'Pinnocchio'; 'Snow White and the Seven Dwarfs'; 'Bambi'; and 'Dumbo' (the baby elephant who could fly with his big flapping ears). We saw also the wonderful new Judy Garland film – 'The Wizard of Oz'.

Other films were in black and white. I loved especially a Roy Rogers film – a singing cowboy with a lovely white horse called Trigger. Another time I was taken to see 'Lassie Come Home' about a lovable collie dog who got lost and had lots of adventures finding her way home.

While the bombing continued relentlessly night after night, everyone was getting more and more furious with the Germans. My Dad liked quoting 'Bomber Harris', the Chief of Bomber Command, who said, "*They've* sown the Wind and *they* will reap the Whirlwind!"

In his book about the terrible raid on the night of 10th/11th May 1941, 'The City That Wouldn't Die', Richard Collier wrote:

"One by one the railway terminals were going . . . St Pancras and Cannon Street by 12.15 . . . at 1.0 Euston and King's Cross, the alternative routes to the north . . . at 1.25 Victoria out, with four unexploded bombs . . . Paddington at 1.15 with an appalling casualty list . . . Liverpool Street, the main line terminal for the east, soon after. All three southern terminals – Charing Cross, London Bridge, Waterloo – were out, too. Only Marylebone remained.

"And this was only the beginning – every river bridge between Lambeth and the Tower of London was blocked or cratered . . . twenty-nine miles of the underground railways were out . . . six telephone

exchanges already gone in the City of London alone . . . all power including the high tension cut off in the South-west Indian Docks . . . Beckton Gas Works, the largest in the world, blown sky-high, and 700 gas mains fractured across the city . . . thousands of streets impassable with fallen buildings."

Next morning, 155,000 families were without gas, electricity or water – over 600 water mains broken.

6. "Don't You Know There's a *War* on?" ~ 1941

My Mum and Dad were keen theatre-goers. When Mum was young she had sung in concerts and still had a lovely soprano voice. At home doing the cooking she sang along to the wireless and knew the words of most of the songs of the day. Her favourites were from Ivor Novello or the Gilbert and Sullivan operas. Now she and Dad sometimes took Frank and me to a Saturday afternoon performance at the London Palladium, or another theatre, to see the famous comedians: Tommy Trinder, Sid Fields, Arthur Askey, Max Wall. Mum always wore her smart navy-blue suit and hat when we went up to the West End. I had to polish my shoes and wear my 'best' clothes.

Once we went to an evening performance and, while the audience was rocking with laughter, the siren went off. An announcement was made from the stage: "Anyone wishing to take cover will be directed to the shelter, but the show will carry on." Hardly anyone moved. Inside the vast, warm, red-plush and gilt auditorium, it seemed the right thing to do was to ignore the heavy booming noises some distance away.

At another performance, someone on stage leant on a lamp-post and sang, 'Maybe it's Because I'm a Londoner . . . ' The backdrop was the skyline of London at night, with a scattering of big white stars over an inky-blue sky and the black silhouette of St Paul's in the foreground. It was then I got my first twinge of understanding of how much Londoners loved their city – especially now.

In 1941 Greta Briggs wrote a poem called 'London Under Bombardment':–

I, who am known as London, have faced stern times before,
have fought and ruled and traded for a thousand years and more;
I knew the Roman legions and the hard-voiced Danish hordes;
I saw the Saxon rebels and blood on the Norman swords;
but, though I am scarred by battle, my grim defenders vow,
never was I so stately, nor so well-beloved as now.
The lights that burn and glitter in the exile's lonely dream,

the lights of Piccadilly, and those that used to gleam
down Regent Street and Kingsway, may now no longer shine,
but other lights are burning and their splendour, too, is mine,
seen in the weary faces and glimpsed in the steadfast eyes,
where English homes lie broken and death descends from the skies.
The bombs have shattered my churches, have torn my streets apart,
but they have not bent my spirit and they shall not break my heart.
My people's faith and courage are the lights of London Town,
which still will shine in legend, though my last great bridge were
    down.

Whenever we went up to the West End I spotted various foreign soldiers around the streets of London, wearing uniforms which were much more interesting than the drab ones worn by our own Tommies.

London was host to many people of different nationalities. During the first German Blitzkrieg, both the Norwegian and the Dutch Royal Families fled to London, as well as the Polish Government-in-Exile. The Polish Air Force contributed four squadrons to fight with the RAF. After Dunkirk there were the Free French and many individual servicemen from other European nations. The first of our Commonwealth troops to arrive were the Canadians, followed later by Australians, New Zealanders, Indians, Gurkhas and South Africans.

I still scooted to school, along the road and round the corner, into the narrow lane cutting through the golf-links between hedges, where I could freewheel downhill, going faster and faster; then over the humpy-back bridge across the New River *(the canal which ran through Enfield)* – sometimes stopping to watch little fluffy ducklings bobbing along in line with their mother leading the convoy – through the empty park and along the road to school, with a final burst of high speed down the steep slope into the playground.

At that time of morning there was usually no-one about in the lane or the park, but a friendly hedger-and-ditcher worked along the lane from time to time. He always said "Hello!" and waved me on my way as I shot past him. Then one day a solitary, large policeman came strolling over the bridge and saw me hurtling towards him. I got a shock when I saw him stop short and hold up his hand. I only just managed to skid to a halt as I reached him and looked up, wondering what was wrong.

"You know, doing that you could bash into somebody. It's a very dangerous thing to do, isn't it?" Struck dumb, I nodded reluctantly. "Now, you won't do it again, will you?" I shook my head vigorously. He smiled and let me go and I carried on slowly, one foot dangling to act as a brake. As I reached the bridge over the river, I looked over my shoulder and saw him looking over *his* shoulder, so I disappeared fast, over the bridge and into the park out of his sight.

> *A new sign at the golf club:-*
> *"Players are asked to collect bomb and shell splinters from fairways to prevent damage to mowing machines;*
> *In competitions during gunfire or while bombs are falling, players may take cover without penalty for ceasing play;*
> *A player whose stroke is affected by the explosion of a bomb or shell, or by machine-gun fire, may play another ball from the same place. Penalty one stroke."*

One day Mum declared she must have a washing machine. She said the neighbours didn't appear to have to put up with the sort of chaos that washday (Monday) always caused in our house. Dad had no peace until he finally made her the proud owner of a second-hand so-called 'automatic' washing machine. The only trouble was that most of the chores connected with it were not very automatic!

First, Mum had to fill the machine with hot water. This meant that the coke boiler fire in the kitchen had to be stoked up until the flames were roaring. Then, when the water was as hot as could be, a hose was connected to the tap over the sink and the water led into the top of the machine. After the automatic washing bit – the machine obligingly vibrating and thumping noisily on the kitchen floor – the water was emptied out by hose from the bottom.

Then the washing had to be hauled out for rinsing in cold water in the sink until, finally, everything had to go through the mangle rollers fixed to the top of the machine, with my Mum puffing and struggling with heavy wet sheets and the whole house smelling of steam and wet washing, just as it always did on washday before we got this wonderful new automatic. *(It was not until some years after the war that Mum finally got what was called a 'Fully Automatic' with a spinner, which transformed her life!)*

If I was around when the neighbours called in, they told a lot of funny stories about bumping into lamp-posts in the blackout; or trying to have a bath in the regulatory five inches of water (even the King and Queen had to do this!); or sitting down to a Sunday dinner with thoughts of roast beef, but having to make do with the offering of scrambled dried egg and chips.

One neighbour told us that he was coming home on a bus when the air raid warning sounded and the bus driver decided to take a frightened old lady all the way home to her front door. Then, trying to find his way back to his official route, the driver got lost in the blackout and had to stop to ask for directions from a passing air raid warden.

We had our own family stories. Mum always busy and complaining, "I've only got *two* pairs of hands!" Frank rushing in excitedly one day, saying, "Some shops are *shut* and some are *closed*!" And so on. But Dad was my main source of entertainment – always ready to predict the most sinister and unlikely things you could imagine. His awful warnings always reduced the pair of us to tears of laughter.

Whenever I couldn't get my own way with Mum, I went to Dad who was more susceptible to my wheedling persuasion, for he never knew whether Mum had forbidden something or other!

Dad taught me the old wartime songs: 'Roll Out the Barrel'; 'It's a Long Way to Tipperary'; and 'Pack up your Troubles in your Old Kit Bag'. I didn't know then that these were the songs he sang in the Great War. For me, they were just the ordinary songs of the day – as Wartime was just the normal state of affairs. My favourite song was: 'Bless 'em All, Bless 'em All, the Long and the Short and the Tall', which we both sang loudly in chorus. This was a new wartime song.

Sometimes I 'helped' Dad in his office with a funny little machine called the addressograph. While I fed the envelopes in, it automatically stamped on the addresses from a tiny conveyor belt of inked cards. I wanted to 'help' with the stencilling machine as well, but Dad put his foot down over that.

Dad never spoke about his experiences in the Great War but he liked bringing up the Boer War in family conversation, no matter what was being talked about. Mum always got exasperated and everyone else teased him. Not the Boer War again, Dad! But there was I believing he'd been a soldier in the Boer War, as well as the Great War, until eventually I found out he was only two years old when the Boer War ended!

The grown-ups were always talking about Wartime. "You can't do that in Wartime!" If you asked for anything you wanted, the answer was always, "No! Don't you know there's a *War* on?" What would Peacetime be like? According to the song there would be bluebirds over the white cliffs of Dover and I liked the picture this brought to mind, but I couldn't imagine life in Peacetime. Secretly I thought it might be rather boring – for one thing there wouldn't be any more wartime songs and jokes.

Dad told me that during the Great War, everyone had said that was the War to end all Wars. Now here we were again . . .

In the first main Blitz, much of London's history over the centuries was lost. The 16th century hall of Gray's Inn, the halls of five ancient livery companies and many beautiful old churches (including eight designed by Christopher Wren), as well as whole sections of street systems in, for example, the Borough of Stepney, were totally obliterated. The famous Guildhall was burned out and Churchill wept when he saw the damage wrought by a high explosive bomb through the roof of the House of Commons. In the centre of the City alone (the area originally settled by the Romans), bombing killed more than 30,000 and injured 40,000.

Gas-masks seemed to have become less important now and I felt confident enough, along with my classmates, to 'forget' to bring mine to school. The teachers appeared to forget about them as well.

I was proud of my good marks for reading and writing, but as time went by we were given very poor-quality exercise books because of the shortage of paper. The new exercise books were made out of thin, blotched paper, which soaked up the ink. *(Perhaps this was the first recycled paper!)* My marks for 'composition' dropped right down, for I stopped bothering to try and was handing in work covered with blots and smudges, very often unfinished.

Eventually I got hauled in front of the headmistress and was given a 'talking-to'. My class teacher procured a new nib for my pen and things got a bit better, especially when I pinched a piece of blotting paper from Dad's office. I even wrote a story about a little girl who had lots of magic adventures and this was praised by the teacher and read by her to the class. But my pride was deflated when the class complained that I hadn't given any details about the three wishes granted at the end of the story – I'd got tired of writing it and brought it to an abrupt end!

My favourite school day was Friday when, in the afternoon, the headmistress read stories aloud to us from books such as Treasure Island, Gulliver's Travels, Robinson Crusoe or Pilgrim's Progress.

These books were chosen not just for their stories but in the hope of encouraging self-reliance. Swift wrote in Gulliver's Travels that a man who can make two ears of corn grow upon a spot of ground where only one grew before would do more for Mankind than the whole race of Politicians put together. And a reviewer wrote: "It follows that to increase the Internal Resources of a Country is the truest means of making it independent, just as to strengthen the Internal Resources of an Individual is the best way to make him able to cope with the world."

7. "Yes! We Have No Bananas"

Sometimes I overheard the BBC News about ships being sunk by enemy torpedoes and the grown-ups talked about cargoes of food lost at the bottom of the ocean. If he couldn't invade our island, Hitler seemed determined to starve us.

With America determinedly neutral, Churchill demanded, "Give us the tools and we will finish the job!" to persuade President Roosevelt to send armaments and food to Britain on 'Lend Lease' – the price to be settled later, since we were rapidly becoming bankrupt fighting the war alone.

As most of the Continent was under occupation and all the British Commonwealth countries at war with Germany, America was Britain's only source of food imports, but there was no let up in the Battle of the Atlantic. Although the ships of our Merchant Navy sailed in convoys, escorted by the Royal Navy for protection, these were constantly under torpedo attack from enemy submarines (U-boats).

In September 1940, the USA sent fifty mothballed First World War destroyers, needing repair and updating, to be used for protecting our convoys; in return Roosevelt secured the right to establish a string of military bases on British territories from Newfoundland down to the Caribbean. ('Blitz' by M.J. Gaskin)

The Royal Navy was equipped with a modern weapon, known as 'Asdic', to detect any lurking U-boat. In 1916, during World War I, British, American and French scientists had set up an Antisubmarine Detection Investigation Committee, ASDIC, which developed a system for detecting underwater objects. This sent out sound waves that rebounded against the object, sending back an echo.

The first I knew about rationing was when Mum announced that the family had to give up sugar in tea. She said she needed the sugar ration for puddings and cakes. I never drank tea then, so it didn't bother me, but Dad couldn't bear unsweetened tea so Mum kept him supplied with saccharines. Dad's tea was very important because every time there was a disaster he said, "Let's have a cup of tea!" and this made everything get better again.

What did upset me was when my butter ration was reduced from four to two ounces a week – that made me really cross with Jerry! To save argument, Mum gave each of us our own little butter dish. Mine was in the shape of a little thatched house, with the roof as lid. I got through most of my butter ration in two or three days and had to eat margarine, which I hated, for the rest of the week. Frank scraped his butter very meanly on the bread and managed to make it last a bit longer. This state of affairs continued for a long time until Mum had the brilliant idea of beating margarine and butter together, with a heavy wooden hammer. *(There were no 'spreadable' varieties, so this must have been hard work!)*

Butter, yes, I missed it badly – but I was not so bothered about the shortage of fresh eggs. We seemed to have plenty of dried egg, which Mum mixed with water and transformed into scrambled egg or used for making batters or cakes, but it was a rare occasion when Frank and I had a fresh shell egg for tea.

For this event Mum provided a personal egg-cup each for Frank and me. Frank's egg-cup was a pretty red cow, mine a yellow chick. I wanted to swap over, but Frank wasn't having any – and this was not the only time he upset me! Frank could never resist teasing 'little sister' and told me, just as I was about to dip my spoon into the egg, that there was a tiny baby chick inside! I laid down the spoon declaring I'd never eat an egg again and poor Frank got a sharp telling-off from Mum.

Mum always took the family ration books along with her to the shops. We each had our own ration book, the pages marked off in 'coupons' for the weekly amount of meat, sugar and so on allowed to each person. Mum had to pass over the ration books with the money so that the shopkeeper could cross out the used coupons.

There were no bananas, oranges or, indeed, any variety of foreign foods throughout the war; the convoys brought only basic commodities such as tea, sugar or tinned meat. By the end of 1940, 728,000 tons of food and animal foodstuffs had been sunk in the Battle of the Atlantic. By the end of the war, 14 million tons of our merchant shipping had been lost (statistics from internet sources).

Enemy spies transmitted details of convoy routes to the German High Command, who then sent this information by coded radio messages to U-boat captains. To warn a convoy to alter its route, it was vital to break the German codes. Thanks to Polish Intelligence officers this was made possible, for they had constructed a copy of the German 'Enigma' coding machine before the war, which they handed over to the British.

Under Churchill's orders, a secret code-breaking station, referred to as Station X, was set up at Bletchley Park, a Victorian mansion in the small railway town of Bletchley, about 50 miles west of Cambridge. All kinds of civilians – mathematicians, crossword-puzzle addicts, linguists and various eccentric intellectuals – were selected and recruited to decipher German codes.

As the enemy changed the settings of the Enigma every day, there were millions of permutations of letters to deal with and Station X worked day and night so that urgent signals could be sent to the Royal Navy, providing them with the co-ordinates of U-boat 'wolf-packs' lying in wait for our convoys.

There were long queues outside shops every time any extra food became available. I got fed up with having to stand in so many different queues every time Mum took me shopping but, despite all my grumbling, if Mum saw an extra long queue she always had to join it in case she missed something.

At David Greig's, the grocer's shop, one counter was a long marble slab with a fierce looking bacon slicing machine. This was operated by a very big man in a white coat who asked you how thick you wanted the slices and wrapped up your ration in greaseproof paper. At another counter the shopping assistant measured out sugar from sacks into one- or two-lb sized dark blue paper bags. When we called at the fishmonger's, he wrapped the raw, wet fish in newspapers.

There were no plastic bags, wrapping or bottles. During and for a long time after the war, drinks were sold in glass bottles and you could get something like 1d or 2d – old pennies – back on every bottle you returned.

Mum stuffed everything into a big canvas bag and extra net bags – she'd got fed up with her old wicker shopping basket which was never big enough for a week's family shopping. Then we walked home, uphill most of the way, carrying the heavy bags. *(After the war my mother acquired a shopping trolley, but my parents never owned a car for all their lives.)*

Every time Mum took me shopping, I begged her to buy some of the bananas hanging up on hooks above the greengrocer's stall outside his shop, but she said, "Those aren't real, they're made of wax." I thought she was just being stingy – they looked so *real*. I desperately wanted a banana and pestered her every time we went to the shops, but she got very irritated and wouldn't listen.

I heard a song on the wireless, which seemed to have been written especially for me. It was meant to be a barrow boy singing in the market:

> *Yes! We have no Bananas.*
> *We have no Bananas today…*

The thought of a ship, loaded with bananas, sinking to the bottom of the ocean, filled me with woe. The best things about Peacetime, I decided, would be butter and bananas!

One day when I came home from school, Mum had a lovely surprise for me. "Here you are – a mashed banana sandwich." Delighted, I ate all of it and asked for more. Later on that day I heard Mum boasting about how she had boiled parsnips until they were soft and mashed them up with drops of the banana essence she used for flavouring cakes. I didn't mind – it tasted just like mashed banana. From then on, Mum was pestered to boil parsnips!

As the deadly Battle of the Atlantic continued, and despite the USA's official position of neutrality, our convoys were joined by American 'Liberty Ships', running the gauntlet of German U-boats alongside the Royal Navy.

A modern BBC television programme about the Atlantic War described how the Royal Navy depth-charged and forced a U-boat to the surface and the German crew abandoned ship so that they could be rescued. Before the U-boat sank, a sub-lieutenant with two sailors managed to board it and recover an Enigma machine and a codebook showing the settings for that month. This gave the cryptologists at Station X a valuable lead. In the year 2000, Hollywood made a film of this exploit with American actors, so a modern audience might not realise this was a British achievement.

In the garden we grew raspberries, gooseberries, runner beans, lettuces and tomatoes. There were also four little fruit trees – eating apple, cooking apple, plum and cherry. Mum bottled quantities of peeled, sliced fruit to store for winter. She kept rows of filled glass jars *(Kilner jars)* at the back of our larder, each with a rubber sealing ring at the top under the glass lid, ready for making pies and puddings. She also made lots of jam – enough for a year – and we went out for walks to collect blackberries in the autumn. There was an old crab apple tree in the middle of the garden, so we had crab apple jelly as an alternative spread.

Whenever Bob (the milkman's horse) left his 'droppings' outside the house, Dad rushed out to shovel them up to use as manure on the garden. Mum was always deeply embarrassed by this – whatever will the neighbours think? – but Dad wasn't going to see good manure going to waste!

As well as the garden, Dad had an allotment on the local golf-links so that he could 'Dig for Victory'. He grew potatoes, carrots, onions, parsnips, cabbages and beetroot. I went along to 'help' him on Saturdays and enjoyed digging out lovely new potatoes.

During the war the UK came the nearest it has ever been to self-sufficiency in food. Common and wasteland, parks and gardens were dug over for growing vegetables. Even part of London's Hyde Park was ploughed over; other parts were needed for anti-aircraft batteries and underground air-raid shelters.

With no imported vegetables or fruit, people ate fresh local produce in season. It has since been acknowledged that the nation was at its healthiest during the 1940s. Farming was still organic, with tasty produce from healthy unadulterated soil. The orchards of Kent, the 'Garden of England', produced scores of varieties of delicious apples (not available today due to EU regulations). But it was during the war years when the first 'intensive farming' started, using new chemical fertilizers and pesticides and with no period of fallow (rest) for exhausted soil to recover.

Mum saw to it that the family never went hungry. With five of us, she was able to use all the family's meat coupons to get a good-sized joint of beef for Sundays, occasionally ringing the changes with lamb or pork. On Mondays, we ate the leftovers cold, with Mum's home made pickles or chutney. Beef provided suet and Mum made mouth-watering suet puddings with fruit to keep us filled. She also 'clarified' the beef dripping, which we salted and spread on bread or toast. This was very tasty, but still, it didn't quite make up for having no butter.

Nearly every day we ate tinned spam *(Specially Processed American Meat)*. Spam sandwiches. Spam with salad. Spam fritters. Spam with chips. Mum, what's for supper? SPAM! I swore an oath *(kept to this day)*: "After the war I will *never* eat spam again." We ate bubble-and-squeak (mashed potato mixed with shredded cabbage and fried hard until it was brown and crispy) with spam or corned beef.

We had no refrigerator but there was a 'cold' tiled shelf in the larder on the north side of the house, with a fine meshed wire cage as a meat safe to protect our weekly joint from flies. In the summer, Mum kept the butter dish and milk bottles cool by storing them in earthenware containers, specially shaped for the job and filled with cold water. She had a funny little rubber gadget for drawing off the cream at the top of the milk to use on fruit salads in summertime.

After the Channel Isles were freed from German occupation at the end of the war, the delicious milk from Jersey or Guernsey cows once more became available. Milk was not homogenised in those days and the rich cream rose to the top. After cream had been drawn off, the remainder was similar to today's semi-skimmed milk but, as it was organic, it was somewhat tastier.

What I liked much better than margarine as a spread was Mum's home made curd cheese. She saved any left-over milk, keeping it until it turned sour and solid, then wrapped it in fine muslin and tied it up over the sink, leaving it to drip and finally salting it when it was ready for spreading. *(Don't try it! Today's milk just turns bad.)*

At school we were each given a small glass bottle of milk at morning playtime – this, we were told, to keep our bones strong. The school bottles were exactly the same shape as the milkman's pint bottles, but smaller, only holding one third of a pint with a little bit of cream at the top. Milk was rationed like everything else, so school milk was a bonus. *The Government also provided free bottles of cod liver oil for babies, which mothers collected from the baby clinics.*

Talking in class was strictly forbidden, but one day I risked whispering to my friend behind me. The teacher marched angrily down the gangway between the desks and gave me a good thumping. It was near the end of the school day and I was still in tears when the bell rang to go home. The same teacher came out to the gate with us and smiled at me, saying, "Goodnight, Patsy." I supposed she wanted to make it up with me, but I refused to answer or look at her while I hauled my scooter out of the shed. With some effort I managed to keep the tears flowing all the way home (a bit difficult, as it was a journey of about 20 minutes, most of it uphill!) because I wanted Mum to feel sorry for me.

Mum sat me by the fire and brought me a helping of blackberry and apple suet pudding, the juice running down on the plate. It was so delicious I wanted a second helping, then another, then another, until I couldn't eat any more. There didn't seem to be much left over for the rest of the family and I had a brief inkling of shame, but felt delightfully warm and comforted.

Coal was also rationed and we had no central heating – very few houses did. To keep ourselves warm, our schoolteacher told us to eat plenty of fat and get plenty of exercise. We went everywhere on foot or on bikes; so did the grown-ups, because there weren't many private cars and in any case petrol was on the ration. Once a week we had an afternoon of P.T. *(Physical Training)* and in the summer term there was a Sports Day with races. *Even with all the bread and dripping and suet puddings, in those days no-one was 'obese'.*

On the News we heard about the Black Market. Some people made profits out of the shortages caused by war and this was thought to be unpatriotic. The Black Market caused further shortages and was unfair to those who could not afford to pay Black Market prices. Rationing was fair to all, rich or poor.

I needed a new dress for school, but Mum had run out of clothing coupons. As well as a ration book of coupons for food, everyone was given a limited number of clothing coupons meant to last for a year. You had to be careful to use these on the bare necessities, for you couldn't get any more until the following year. Mum took an old pair of Dad's trousers and worked magic with her sewing machine. I went off to school in a new grey wool dress made in panels, the latest fashion, decorated with red rick-rack.

The teacher, who was in on the secret, was talking to us about 'Make Do and Mend', a wartime slogan. She asked me to stand up in front of the class, so that she could tell the other children that my mother had made a dress out of . . . She hesitated and finished off with " . . . something." I guessed she didn't want to embarrass me, but she needn't have worried. I only wanted to boast to my classmates about *my* mother being the cleverest!

When we did have clothing coupons to spend, Mum took me on a shopping trip to Pearsons, the big drapers' store in Enfield Town. There were high-seated chairs at the counters, where Mum would sit and discuss her requirements with the shop assistant. This shop was where I liked watching the little cash-cylinder whizz across the ceiling. The shop assistant behind the counter took Mum's money and put it with the bill into a little hollow wooden cylinder attached on two wheels to an overhead cable. Then she pulled a lever, so that the cylinder whizzed along the cable into the cashier's kiosk, a small glass partition reached by a flight of steps. The cashier took out the bill and the money, put in the right change and sent the little cylinder whizzing back again.

We hardly ever bought ready-made clothes. Mum's purchases were more often of material and paper patterns for dressmaking. She spent hours crawling round the living-room floor, cutting out and pinning, usually to make dresses for me to wear at school as I was growing so fast. She also turned sheets sides to middle as they wore out and spent evenings mending clothes or darning socks.

Dad had to go to Dublin on trade union business. He travelled by ferry across the Irish Sea and Mum spent the time worrying until he got back safely again, bringing with him a pound of rich salty Irish butter and a thick slab of milk chocolate which, he told me, he'd smuggled out in his socks! Dad could never be serious when he talked to me. *Eire was a neutral country and not subject to rationing, but just as dependent as we were upon our convoys for supplies.*

We had a feast. It was the first time I'd tasted milk chocolate. I'd had no sweets since rationing began because Mum exchanged all the family's sweet coupons *(two ounces per person per week)* for extra sugar to make jam, cakes and puddings.

Britain was saved from the threat of starvation by the Government's introduction of rationing and the Dig for Victory campaign; and particularly by the enemy code breaking achievement at Bletchley Park, which was not only crucial to the war generally but vital in the Battle of the Atlantic, where the loss of convoys carrying food supplies threatened our survival.

One who worked at Bletchley Park was the genius, Alan Turing, famous for the first electro-mechanical computer, the Turing Machine. An engineer named Tommy Flowers from the Post Office Research Station at Dollis Hill in London had also arrived at Station X. Inspired by Turing's work, he built the world's first programmable electronic computer, nicknamed 'Colossus'. This made a breakthrough in the speed of deciphering the enemy's coded signals to U-boats.

After the Americans joined the war at the end of 1941, Alan Turing acted as a link between US and British Intelligence, but was not permitted to divulge all the advances made by the British.

At the end of the war Churchill ordered the records at Bletchley Park to be burnt and Colossus to be destroyed. Using microchip technology a decade later, the Americans developed a computer, which they claimed incorrectly to be the first, since the work at Bletchley Park remained secret until 1975.

8. "It's That Man Again!"

Mum always switched on the wireless in the morning and left it on all day so that the family never missed the News or any speeches by Churchill.

NEWS: "Here is the Nine o'Clock News and this is Alvar Liddell reading it."

My bedtime was between 8 and 9 o'clock, but during the war we lived by 'double summertime' to help the farmers, so it was only 6 or 7 o'clock by the sun. I often wheedled Dad into letting me stay up until the BBC Nine O'Clock News – I insisted on holding out until the ninth and last DONG of Big Ben had died away and sometimes managed to stay even longer.

Between news bulletins in the daytime there were musical or comedy programmes to cheer people up. 'Workers' Playtime' was one of these – music and jokes to entertain factory workers as they constructed planes, tanks, guns, etc.

Sometimes there were talks, such as advice to housewives on how to make a tasty meal on wartime rations, but for most of the day we lived to a background of songs and big band music.

The BBC, the only British broadcaster at that time, played a big part in our lives. There were only two BBC channels, the Home Service and the World Service, until the Light Programme started in 1945. As well as keeping people informed with news bulletins, the BBC's most important function was to be a jaunty voice keeping up morale.

There were no phone-in programmes for problems or counselling; no-one had heard of 'stress' and, in any case, it was 'Not Done' to complain about your lot!

On the wireless we heard romantic songs: 'The Last Time I Saw Paris', 'They Can't Black Out the Moon', 'A Nightingale Sang in Berkeley Square', 'Begin the Beguine' and 'Lily Marlene':[1]

---

[1] Originally a German song *Lili Marleen*, whose haunting tune was written by Norbert Schultze in 1939 to words written by Hans Leip in 1915. It became popular

Underneath the lamplight,
By the barracks gate,
Darling, I remember
The way you used to wait.
T'was there that you whispered
Tenderly
That you loved me,
Would always be
My Lily of the Lamplight,
My own Lily Marlene . . .

And patriotic songs: 'There'll Always Be An England'; 'I Vow to Thee My Country'; 'Land of Hope and Glory'; 'London Pride'; and 'The White Cliffs of Dover', sung by Vera Lynn:

There'll be bluebirds over
The white cliffs of Dover,
Tomorrow,
Just you wait and see.
There'll be love and laughter,
And Peace ever after
Tomorrow,
When the world is free.

The shepherd will flock his sheep,
The valley will bloom again,
And Jimmy will go to sleep
In his own little room again.

There'll be bluebirds over . . . .

And comic songs: 'Kiss Me Goodnight, Sergeant Major'; 'Don't Let's Be Beastly to the Germans'; 'In Der Fuhrer's Face'; 'Who do you think you are kidding, Mr. Hitler?'; 'Run, Rabbit, Run!'

---

with British Eighth Army soldiers serving in North Africa when they heard it broadcast on German radio and adopted it as their own. The first English version was recorded by Anne Shelton singing with the Ambrose Orchestra and it went on to be recorded by many others, the best known being Marlene Dietrich, who recorded versions in both German and English in 1943.

I felt sorry for the poor little rabbit, but somehow didn't connect this with Mum's delicious rabbit pie. A comic on the wireless put new words to this tune:

'Run, Adolph, Run, Adolph, Run, Run, Run!
See what you've Been, Gone and Done, Done, Done!'

There was also a lot of rousing military brass band music, which always left me feeling absolutely confident that *we* would win the war!

Then there was Victor Sylvester's programme of dance music for couples learning how to dance, beginning with the signature tune and Victor Sylvester chanting, "Slow, Slow, Quick-Quick Slow…"

Twiddling with the tuning knob on the wireless, I often came across the sound of rapid bleeps – Morse Code. I tried to learn the Morse Code from my brother's Scout Book, but there was no way I could keep up with the speed on the wireless.

I was particularly intrigued by a low, mysterious drum signal heard on the wireless every now and again: Bom-Bom-Bom-BOMMM. This was sometimes followed by the announcement, 'Ici Londres!' *(This is London!)*, when various statements were read out in French. Dad told me the drum sound was the Morse signal for V, which stood for Victory. Later I found out that this was a call to the French Resistance to listen to instructions or information in a secret code – invented family messages or quotations from poetry.

On the Continent, German occupying forces banned listening to the BBC, but this regulation was widely disobeyed. The BBC News was trusted to be generally more reliable than the propaganda output from European stations controlled by Germany. Resistance movements across Europe relied on the BBC World Service for information or coded messages.

The French Resistance listened to the BBC on hidden radio-receivers and transmitted messages to London arranging for British agents or weapons to be dropped by parachute. They risked capture and torture by the Gestapo (the Nazi secret police) or betrayal by the French civilian police, who worked for the German occupying authorities, or for the new Vichy Government (established with German agreement in the south of France), and who took part in the forced transportation of French Jews 'to the East'.

In the long winter evenings we sat around the coal fire, making toast over the flames with a long-handled brass fork while we listened to the entertainment on the wireless: 'In Town Tonight'; 'Much Binding in the Marsh'; 'ITMA' ('It's That Man Again'). 'ITMA' was introduced with a bouncy jingle:

> 'It's that Man again, it's that Man again,
> Yes, it's Tommy Handley, it's Him.
> When trouble's brewing, it's his doing,
> That Man . . . that Man again!'

When the siren went off one of us would always say, "It's that *Man* again!" but *we* meant Hitler! There was another saying from 'ITMA', which most people used instead of Good-Bye: 'TTFN', meaning 'Ta-Ta For Now!'

Dad and I really enjoyed ITMA with its characters of Mrs Mopp: "Can I do you now, sir?" and Cecil and Claude: "After you, Cecil. No. After *you*, Claude!" This came in very useful among those staggering about in the blackout!

Then there was Funf, the German spy on the telephone: "This is Funf speaking," and Colonel Chinstrap: "I don't mind if I do!" Tommy Handley was the Minister of Aggravation and Mysteries from the House of Twerps; and Mona Lott was always complaining!

Another comic started off just like my Dad, "Now, the day War broke out," and went on, ". . . my Missus said to me, "*What* are you going to *do*?"

And when Britain 'Stood Alone' the comics sang a new song with the words: "And we'll all go Marching Forward with our Backs against the Wall."

One programme was introduced with the song:

> 'It's 'Monday Night at Eight' o'Clock.
> Can't you hear the chimes?
> They're telling you to take an easy chair.
> Settle by the fireside, take out the Radio Times,
> for 'Monday Night at Eight' is on the air.'

And another song went on running through my head:

> 'We Three, in Happydrome,
> working for the Bee…Bee…Cee,
> Ramsbottom . . .and Enoch . . .and Mee…ee…ee.'

On a BBC television documentary some time after the war, an ex-member of the Hungarian Resistance said that every time he or his friends tuned in to the BBC to get information, they invariably picked up the sound of audiences laughing. "What is it with these English? Are they not fighting a war? Have they all gone mad?"

The comedians on the wireless were always poking fun at the enemy and I thought this must really infuriate the Germans. It was through all the comic songs and jokes I got to know that Hitler and the Nazis believed the Germans were the Master Race who ought to rule over all the other nations! According to Dad, Hitler was jealous, and at the same time admiring, of our little island governing so much of the world. Hitler had said, "Give me a free hand in Europe and I will let you keep your Empire." Huh!

I often heard the 'Home Front' mentioned on the wireless. At first I thought this just meant 'Doing your Bit' to help win the war, but Dad said this was the first war between so-called 'civilized' nations in which ordinary people at home were deliberately targeted by the enemy and in as much danger as soldiers on the Front Line.

Sometimes Lord Haw-Haw's malicious tones broke through the airwaves, drawling, "Jairmany Calling, Jairmany Calling." He told us to give up because Germany was winning all the battles, Germany would win the war, England was finished. Dad told me that Lord Haw-Haw was a British traitor broadcasting from Germany, whose purpose was to lower our morale. We all thought he was absurd – as absurd as Hitler was when he made one of his speeches, shouting, ranting and spluttering with rage.

On the wireless the comedians chanted:

> 'Lord Haw-Haw, the Humbug of Hamburg,
> The Comic of Eau de Cologne!'

Lord Haw-Haw's real name was William Joyce, a naturalized American citizen who had been brought up in Ireland. He was caught by the Allies in Germany in 1945, tried, convicted and hanged for treason.

America was still officially neutral. Joseph Kennedy, Ambassador, had told the British Government at the outset: "Our boys are not going to die in any European war!" This was the view of the Isolationists, widespread across the USA, who doubted that Britain could withstand Germany's assault and had no intention of fighting on the losing side.

However, the Americans later admired us for our success against the odds in the Battle of Britain and our resistance during the Blitz.

Whenever the family was sitting around the fire listening to the wireless, Mum invariably wanted one of us to hold a skein of wool over outstretched arms so that she could wind it up into balls for knitting. She knitted madly every spare moment – socks, jumpers, gloves for us and baby clothes for other people.

Sitting still with arms stretched out was so tedious that Frank, who was having woodworking classes at school, decided to make a wool-winding machine. He constructed a narrow wooden upright frame standing on its own base with two rollers, one at the top and one at the bottom, fixed in place by inserting the axles into two pairs of holes in the frame. Now Mum could stretch the skein of wool over the rollers and sit winding independently, leaving us free to get on with our own hobbies.

Frank often sat on the floor, building various models out of Meccano. One Christmas he was given a little working engine for making moving models such as cars and cranes. He also made Airfix models of aeroplanes, which he hung across the ceiling in his room.

Like most boys, Frank was building up a stamp collection, mainly British or from the British Empire. I watched him using tweezers to arrange these stamps in albums with little sticky hinges. I thought foreign stamps were much prettier than the British ones. Also, they showed the name of the country, so why didn't we? Dad told me this was because the British had introduced the first postal service to the world and the silhouette of our monarch's head was recognised worldwide.

I spent a lot of time reading or drawing pictures, but sometimes I managed to persuade the others to join in a family board game: Snakes and Ladders, Ludo, Sorry; or a game of cards: Snap, Happy Families or Sevens. Quite often Dad was the only one who was willing. Then he and I played Cribbage or Draughts, until he eventually taught me to play Chess – and sometimes let me win!

9. Land of Hope and Glory

One of the first things we learned at school was that the 'Great' of 'Great Britain' indicated the number of islands included in the British Isles – as 'Greater London' indicated London's suburbs. *People still often used the term 'the British Isles' instead of 'the United Kingdom', although Eire had become an independent republic in the 1920s.*

Our teachers told us that as an island race we were, above all, a sea-faring nation. We had developed navigation across the oceans, invented the compass, chronometer and sextant and established Greenwich Mean Time; and we had the largest merchant marine in the world *(four times that of the USA)*, protected by a powerful Royal Navy *(unequalled by any other nation until the USA achieved parity in the 1920s).*

We learned that our island stood on rich coal seams and iron ore deposits, which led us to develop a prosperous manufacturing base. The seas around us served as our protection as well as bountiful fishing grounds. The Gulf Stream, a great current of warm water coming across the Atlantic Ocean from the Gulf of Mexico, warmed our shores, favouring us with a 'temperate' climate. The rainfall made our soil fertile, our land 'green and pleasant'.

We felt blessed. *(It was an age of innocence.)*

We accepted the word 'patriotism' as meaning love of our country and our people, an extension of family love – 'The Dearest and the Best.'

> *"I travelled among unknown men, in lands beyond the sea;*
> *Nor, England, did I know till then what love I bore for thee."*
> **William Wordsworth**

Dad impressed on me that Britain had not been invaded since the Battle of Hastings in 1066. The narrow strip of sea between Britain and the Continent had saved us many times in history from attempted invasions by the Dutch, French and Spanish (so, thought I, it would protect us from the Germans!). He told me that the Bill of

Rights *(1689)* stated that we should never be ruled by 'foreign powers'.

Dad also told me that we were protected from infections such as rabies, which affected the Continent but could not cross the Channel. *Europe was usually called 'the Continent' in those days. A typical British newspaper headline was: 'Continent cut off by Fog!'*

My Dad was keen to make sure I understood that ours was the Mother of Parliaments. The Magna Carta *(originally signed in 1215)* had introduced to the world for the first time the concept of freedom and the rights of an individual against a ruling power. He told me that we abided by an unwritten constitution and our system of law and justice was respected throughout the world. We didn't suffer from revolutions like those that happened abroad and we were the only nation in the world to be served by an unarmed police force, which foreign visitors remarked on with admiration.

On the 24th May the school celebrated Empire Day, when we were taken to a special service at St Andrew's Church in the morning. Then we assembled in the playground to raise the flag and sing 'The Recessional', a poem written by Rudyard Kipling to remind people of their responsibilities as citizens of the Mother Country.

Kipling's message then was understood as similar to that of the proverb, 'Pride goes before a Fall' – a warning against imperial arrogance. We still use Kipling's words, 'Lest we forget', to remember those who sacrificed their lives for their country and those who were murdered by the Germans in the Jewish Holocaust.

Churchill often mentioned the British Empire in his speeches, so by this time I knew that it was not just our own little island which was threatened by the enemy.

In his plan to dominate the European continent, Hitler had formed a pact, called the Axis, with Mussolini, dictator of Italy, who himself had grandiose plans to establish a new Roman Empire around the East Mediterranean and in North Africa.

Among the British territories threatened were the Mediterranean islands of Gibraltar, Malta and Cyprus, all vital bases for the Royal Navy. In Palestine the British were mandated by the League of Nations to keep order, by keeping apart warring factions of Arabs and Jews; in Irak the British governed on behalf of the Arab nations; and in Egypt they administered by request and protected the Suez Canal, jointly owned by Britain and France, which was the shortest route to India, an important part of the British Empire.

The Japanese had been waging war against China since 1937 and in 1940, with the agreement of the French Vichy Government, they occupied French Indo-China (now Vietnam) and became the third Axis Power. Their intention to build an empire over East and South-East Asia, and to claim for themselves the Pacific islands belonging to Great Britain, France or America, threatened the far-eastern parts of the British Empire – India, Burma, Hong Kong, Singapore, Malaya and Borneo – as well as the kingdom of Siam (now Thailand).

At school it was impressed upon us that we had not set out to conquer but the empire had originated and grown in a haphazard way, as a result of expeditions by our famous explorers into unknown and undeveloped parts of the world during previous centuries, followed by the setting up of various local administrations to trade across the oceans in sugar, rubber and tea. All this had laid the foundations of the largest Empire and Commonwealth in history, covering two-fifths of the world. It was known as the empire on which 'the sun never set' because it encircled the globe.

We were told that as the empire developed the aims of the British were to bring law and order where there was violence, education where there was ignorance and medicine where there was disease.

The British built and managed the infrastructure required by an undeveloped society, such as roads, bridges, railways, law courts, schools, universities and hospitals. They also made efforts to bring an end to cruel cultural practices, such as human sacrifice, witchcraft, female infanticide, mutilation for thieving and stoning for adultery.

And we learned that Australia, New Zealand, South Africa and Canada were British Dominions, independently governed – Canada originally populated by those who remained loyal to the Crown during the American Revolution against British rule in our first colonies. The rest of the empire consisted of Protectorates and Colonies scattered over the Middle East, Africa and Asia; and numerous islands dotted across the oceans, which provided coaling stations for our Merchant and Royal Navies.

"We seem, as it were, to have conquered and peopled half the world in a fit of absence of mind." (Sir John Robert Seeley, d.1895)

To begin with, my idea of the world was that Jerry was the Enemy and it would always be Wartime. But now I understood we were a Mother Country of a family of nations and I wondered why our enemies thought they had any hope of winning the war against us when we had all the countries of the Empire and Commonwealth on our side.

In his book, 'Blitz', M J Gaskin writes:
"... 300 vacancies in the Indian Air Reserve attracted 18,000 would-be volunteers ... there were, overall, more volunteers from [India] than could be accommodated in Empire forces at present.

"The hard-pressed RAF also received gifts, ranging from 328 binoculars and telescopes, 'salvaged' by the Boy Scouts of the West Indies for its Observer Corps, to a squadron of Spitfires paid for by the people of Basutoland.

"Other presents to Britain included £300 to the children of London from the children of Mauritius; at a reception in battered Buckingham Palace just before Christmas [1940], thirty-five canteen vans to feed Britain's homeless, all gifts from the Empire, had been presented to Queen Elizabeth [later the Queen Mother].

"In total, the Colonies and Dominions had so far donated around £17 million, mostly in individual gifts, to the fight against Nazism."

Dad told me that India was called 'the Jewel in the Crown' in Victorian times and that the British governed in co-operation with local Indian monarchs of different states.

In the modern Indian Army, soldiers of Sikh, Moslem and Hindu faiths were all united in loyalty to the British. The Gurkhas (Nepalese soldiers) had also been proudly loyal since the early 1800s. In Queen Victoria's time they called themselves 'the Queen's Soldiers'.

Dad was fond of quoting Rudyard Kipling's poem, "You're a better man than I am, Gunga Din!" And at school our teacher read to us 'The Jungle Book' written by Kipling about a little boy Mowgli, left in the Indian jungle and brought up by a family of wolves. I pictured India in my mind and thought, "One day, I shall go there!"

I got an even clearer picture and wanted even more to go to India after Mum took me to see the film 'Sabu, the Elephant Boy' about a young Indian boy who loved his own special elephant. When Sabu wanted to ride, this elephant picked him up in his trunk and swung him over his head to sit on his back.

It was my Dad, the Trade Unionist, who told me with some pride that Great Britain was called the Workshop of the World and that a product stamped 'Made in Great Britain' was recognized as one of the highest quality ("Sterling quality"). The discoveries of our scientists and our inventions and engineering achievements had begun the Industrial Revolution *(which was commonly believed to be one of the finest human achievements).*

With the discovery of the power of steam, the British were the first to build railways, both in our island and across the empire. The Himalayan Railway is still in use today, pulled by the original steam locomotive manufactured in Manchester and running daily up the mountains to Darjeeling.

The Royal Navy exported other scientific and technical achievements around the globe, bringing the modern world into existence. Niall Ferguson, historian at Harvard University, has published a book: 'Empire, How Britain Made the Modern World' – Penguin Group, 2007.

When Dad was talking to Frank and me about the Spitfire, he told us about an international air-race of recently designed sea-planes.

This was the Schneider Trophy competition in the 1920s between the leading industrial powers – Great Britain, France, Italy and the USA. Germany could not enter due to the provisions of the Versailles Treaty after the Great War.

Dad said we had won the air-race three times running using a Rolls-Royce designed engine. This meant we gained the Schneider Trophy outright; the competition ended; and it was this engine, further developed by Rolls-Royce and named the Merlin, which was used by the designer of the Spitfire, Reginald Mitchell.

In the 1930s there was also a competition for the fastest Atlantic crossing between Germany, France, Italy and Great Britain. The trophy was called the Blue Riband and again Britain held the Blue Riband most of the time with the Cunard Liners, such as the Mauritania and the Queen Mary.

Another thing I learned from Dad was that we had introduced most sports, particularly football and cricket, to other nations, along with our sense of 'Team Spirit' and 'Fair Play' – concepts very dear to the hearts of the British.

And, like most children, I gradually absorbed the traditional view of our national characteristics: 'A Stiff Upper Lip' (under-statement in the face of disaster or tragedy); 'A Gentleman's Word is his Bond' (honour); 'The Englishman's Home is his Castle' (the belief that privacy was sacrosanct); 'Live and Let Live' (tolerance); 'Freedom of Speech' (and opinion!); eccentricity; and a famously self-deprecating sense of humour.

I took for granted that we would win the war. I had no doubts on that score. After all, as Dad told me, the British were in the habit of losing every battle except the last!

Evacuees talk to train driver (Getty Images)

At the start of the war trainloads of children left London for safer areas and many families were separated. All the trains had steam locomotives. Passengers would often greet the driver before their journey and say 'thank you for a safe journey' after alighting.

Evacuees on train, 'third class' (Corbis)

On holiday at St Osyth in 1939, Frank and me. (Personal collection)

Our beach bungalow at St Osyth. (Personal collection)

Auntie Louie and me on my fifth birthday. (Personal collection)

Me with evacuee children at Cuffley. (Personal collection)

Barbed wire on the beaches, which were also mined. (Imperial War Museum)

Mum was delighted with our new home at Ridings Avenue, Autumn 1940. (Personal collection)

An Anderson shelter like the one in our garden. We slept on bunk beds on the walls. There was no heating but I never noticed the cold or damp, only the smell of stale earth. (Imperial War Museum)

Second evacuation in 1940; this time by bus. (Getty Images)

Many children had returned from the first evacuation during the 'phoney war' but when the Blitz started in earnest, a second, larger evacuation took place and many families were separated for 'the duration'.

WHY AREN'T THERE MORE TRAINS?

Factories turning out guns, bombers and fighters depend on the Railways for supplies.

To keep them working at top pressure the Railways must run thousands of additional goods trains by day and night.

The Railways must also keep the Nation's food, coal and export trades moving.

Essential trains must have first claim on the lines. It is as vital to ration trains as it is to ration food. The Railways are giving you every passenger train the tracks will take.

WE'LL BEAT HITLER BY HELPING ONE ANOTHER

BRITISH RAILWAYS

1940s newspaper clipping. (Personal collection)

Barrage balloons over London. (Imperial War Museum)

Advertisement offering blackout signs for shops.

Searchlights criss-crossing the night sky, searching for enemy aircraft.. (Personal Collection)

1940s newspaper clipping, recruitment advertisement encouraging women to operate the barrage balloons.

1940s newspaper clipping (Personal collection)

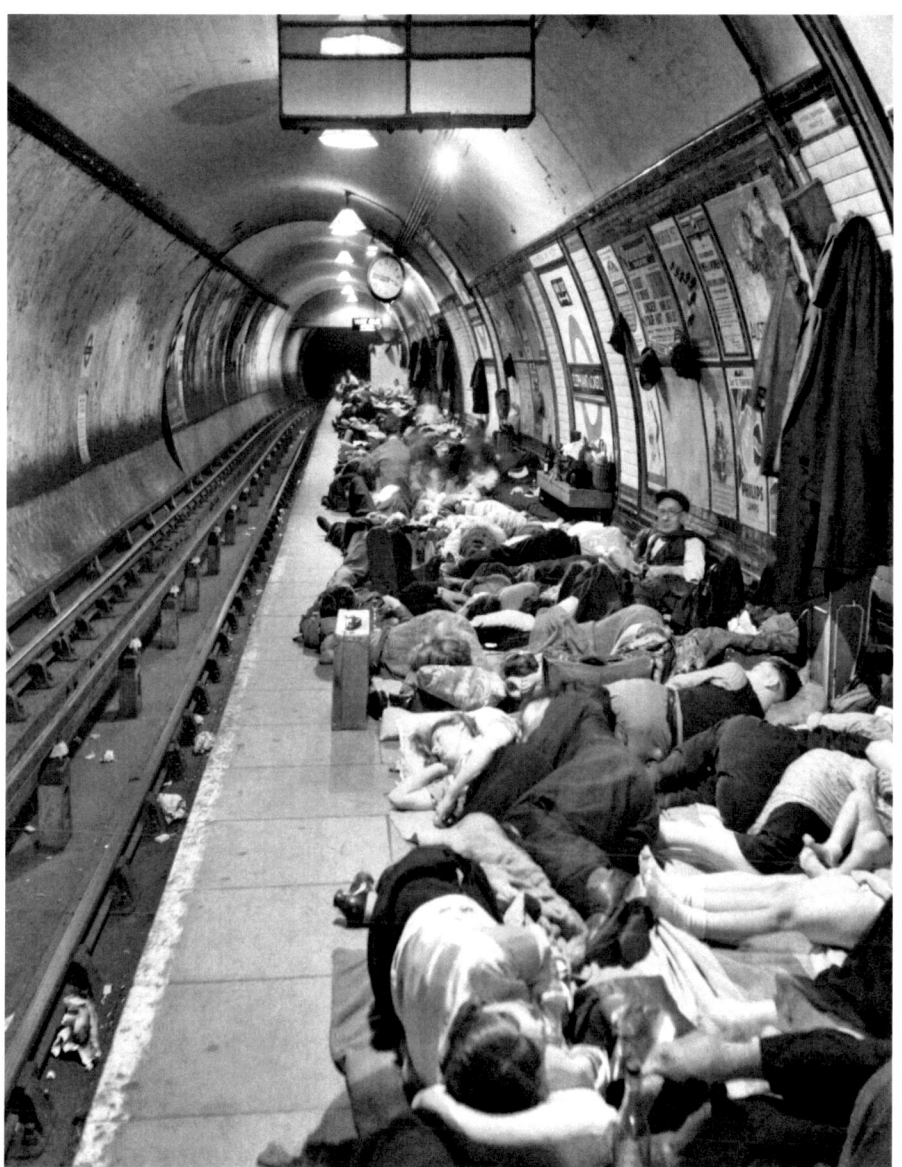

East Enders sleeping in a tube station. (Imperial War Museum)

Policemen escorting pedestrians past a UXB. (Corbis)

A London bus that has fallen into a bomb crater. (Imperial War Museum)

Famous photo of St Paul's Cathedral amid the flames, taken on 29th December 1940 by Herbert Mason of the *Daily Mail*. My dad and I stood on our balcony looking south towards central London, the sky glowing orange with fire. (Corbis)

Bank tube station smashed by a bomb. Behind it the Royal Exchange is displaying a 'Dig for Victory' banner. (Corbis)

A milkman does his round after a raid. (Corbis)

'Back as soon as we beat Hitler' (Corbis)

A postman collects the mail amid the rubble. (Getty Images)

My brother Frank in Scout uniform. (Personal collection)

Morrison shelter (Imperial War Museum). One of the Scouts' 'good deeds was to help people assemble their Morrison shelters.

How the railways used to be. (BBC Hulton Picture Library)

Ticket collector.

Porter.

Guard.

Signalman.

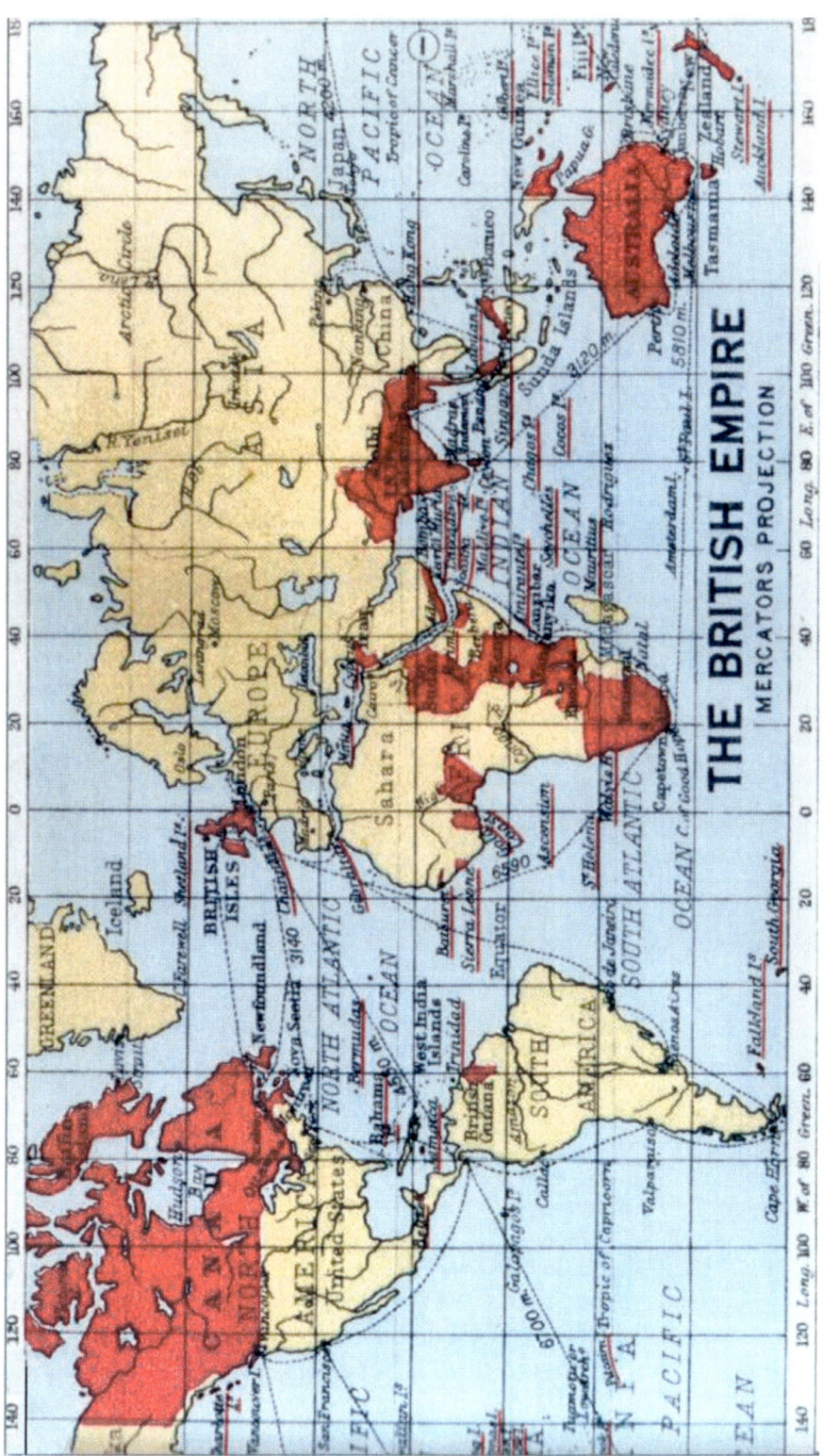
School atlas map of the British Empire.

Poster advertising trips to South Africa & Rhodesia.

Poster advertising London-Paris service.

Poster advertising P&O sailings to Australia.

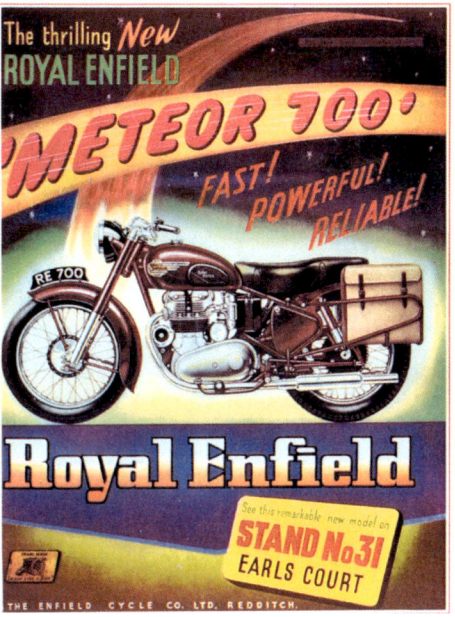

Poster announces the latest Royal Enfield motorbike.

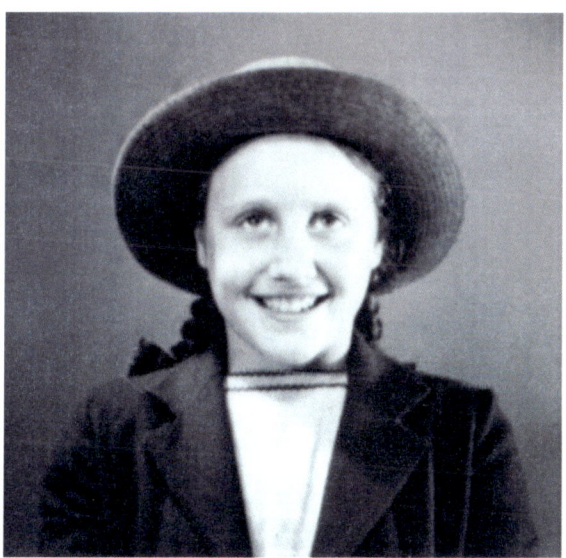

Me, aged seven, in 1941.
(Personal collection)

Cousin John in RAF uniform.
(Personal collection)

Sister Barbara in Wrens uniform.
(Personal collection)

The Doodlebugs started falling in June 1944, shortly after D-Day.
(Imperial War Museum)

An air raid warden rescues a child after a Doodlebug hit. (Corbis)

My brother with Mum on the rocky beach at Combe Martin (Personal collection)

Combe Martin in 1944. (Personal collection)

A London housewife entertaining American GIs. (Corbis)

V.E. Day 8th May 1945 ~ The Royal Family and Churchill acknowledge the vast crowd gathered outside Buckingham Palace. (Getty Images)

V.E. Day outside Buckingham Palace. I was in the crowd, sitting on Dad's shoulders, when the King and Queen and Mr Churchill appeared on the balcony.
(Getty Images)

Visit to my old school (Enfield County School for Girls) in 2001.
(Personal collection)

Enfield public swimming pool, where we went for lessons in the 1940s.
(Personal collection)

Me, aged 11 in 1946, in school uniform. (Personal collection)

Family photograph 1946. (Personal collection)
From left to right: Dad, Barbara, Mum, Frank, Uncle Jack and Me.

Frank in Egypt on National Service in 1947.
(Personal collection)

Frank in Egypt with Egyptian boy Abdul. (Personal collection)

Barbara and Tadek's wedding reception, in our garden at Riding's Avenue
(Personal collection)

Me at 15 in 1949. (Personal collection)

Frank at the piano. He could hear a tune and play it by ear. (Personal collection)

Frank's first car and our dog Doric. (Personal collection)

Cousin Clem, a schoolmaster, who made a school film with my friend Jenny and me. (Personal collection)

1950s programmes from my personal collection.

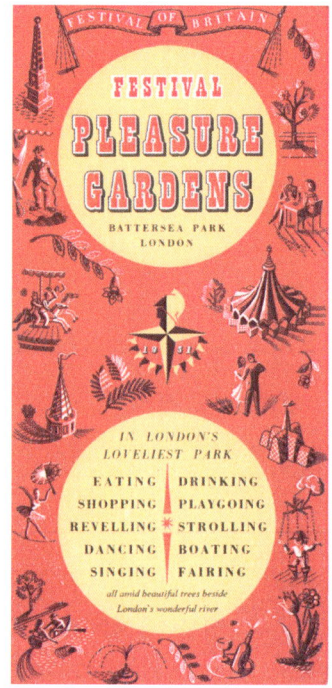

San Sebastian Bay (Personal collection)

Taken by Bambi of me with our Spanish boyfriends. (Personal collection)

Spanish Bullring. (Personal collection)

Me, age 17, a student at the French Institute. Taken by a Polish architectural student in Hyde Park. (Personal collection)

The Natural History Museum in South Kensington. (Personal collection)

My friends and I considered it to be one of the most beautiful buildings in London but the Polish students we used to meet in the museum gardens said it was "wedding cake architecture".

10. The Big Three ~ 1941/42

At school Barbara made friends with a German girl, one of the 10,000 Jewish children brought over to England before the war to escape Nazi persecution. Truda (Gertrud) had been taken in by a Quaker family and had herself become a Quaker.

Barbara brought Truda home to meet Mum and Dad. My Mum was always hospitable – there were times when she even had the milkman in for a cup of tea – so Truda was invited to stay with us and share Barbara's bedroom. Truda was very happy to move in with us and stayed until the end of the war. She became part of the family, another 'big sister' for me, but as a foreign national she had to report to Enfield Police Station once a week.

One evening Mum left the light on upstairs, forgetting to draw the blackout curtains, and someone knocked on the door. *"Put That Light Out!"* Mum was a bit worried afterwards in case people had been suspicious about the 'signal' glaring out into the blackness from the top of the hill where we lived, for all the neighbours knew we were 'harbouring' a German!

- *NEWS: Germany attacks Russia!*

In June 1941, Hitler betrayed the pact he had made with Stalin. German forces swept into Russia taking the Red Army by surprise, slaughtering civilians and burning down villages. Churchill, despite his long-held distrust of the Soviet Union, declared that Russia had now become 'our Enemy's Enemy' and thus, by default, our Ally. He and the Polish Government-in-Exile, who had escaped through Rumania to France and then to London, put pressure on the dictator Stalin to allow the Poles to make their way out of Soviet-occupied territory and to form an army under British command in Palestine.

British convoys now had another perilous journey to make past the north of the British Isles and through stormy seas to Murmansk to keep the Russians supplied with armaments. The Germans attacked our convoys with torpedoes and bombs. Many ships were sunk and nearly 3,000 sailors' lives lost in the icy waters approaching the Arctic Seas.

Dad's face was always serious when he listened to the News on the wireless, but grown-up worries were beyond me. I called round to see the other children in the road, or they came to me. We were a gang of four, all more or less the same age and always in and out of each other's gardens, or using our skipping ropes in the street. If parents were out, back doors were left open for us to come and go as we pleased.

On my 7th birthday when I woke up there were a few little parcels and one large box waiting for me on the breakfast table. Opening the box carefully, I heard a little miaow – and there was a tiny white kitten with blue eyes. He was the present for which I had clamoured, in the face of Mum's reluctance. I was thrilled when the tiny animal came staggering over the table towards me.

The kitten was so pretty I wanted to give him a pretty name and chose Tinker Bell, the name of the fairy in the book Peter Pan. I was forgetting that Tinker Bell was a girl fairy, so the kitten's name soon became shortened to Tinker.

We hadn't heard about tins of catfood in those days and I never thought about how cats were fed. I just hated the smell at the fishmongers when Mum took me there on her shopping trips. My main contribution to Tinker's comfort was to give him a saucer of milk when Mum was not around. I didn't want Tinker to be deprived just because milk was on the ration.

The cat next door was called Bingo. Mrs Britten always called him into the house at night in case of an air-raid and Mum did the same for Tinker. In bed one night in the Morrison shelter, I heard Frank in the kitchen shouting at Mum: "How d'you expect me to concentrate on my homework with all that blasted TINGing going on? What with *her* next door going "BING, BING, BING!" and *you* at the back going "TING, TING, TING!" everyone down the road must think you're *mad!* Frank came out, banging the door, and there was no more TINGing from Mum. Perhaps she couldn't say anything as she was trying not to laugh.

Every evening the grown-ups listened to the BBC Nine-o'Clock News.

- *NEWS: The Ark Royal aircraft carrier sunk by enemy action.*

The British had been the first to pioneer aircraft carriers and the Ark Royal was famous. In November 1941 she was escorting a convoy of ships carrying vital supplies to the island of Malta, a British base, and was first attacked by enemy bombers, then torpedoed by U-boats.

- **NEWS: Pearl Harbour has been attacked by Japanese planes!**

Japan made no declaration of war but, on 7th December 1941, torpedo bombers, launched from Japanese aircraft carriers, attacked the American naval base at Pearl Harbour (in Hawaii), destroying most of the battleship fleet and killing hundreds of sailors. Outraged, the USA immediately declared war against Japan and prepared to send their submarines and aircraft-carriers against the Japanese Navy. What became known as the Pacific War would engage huge numbers of American forces from 1942 until 1945.

In support of his Axis partner, Hitler then declared war on the USA.

To Churchill's relief, the New World had finally been provoked into military action on the side of the Old. Churchill now had to persuade the Americans – whose immediate concern was Japan – that it was vital to defeat "Germany first!"

The USA turned its immense industrial capacity to war and became the prime arsenal for the Allied Powers, who became known as the Big Three: Great Britain with its Empire and Commonwealth; the USSR; and the USA. These were augmented by the Polish Army under British command and by the 'Free French' soldiers rescued from Dunkirk and under the command of their own General de Gaulle in London, who had escaped by plane to England when the French Government capitulated.

- **NEWS: Two British battleships sunk by Japanese torpedo bombers.**

On 10th December 1941, Japanese torpedo bombers attacked two of our most famous battleships, HMS Prince of Wales and HMS Repulse, off the shores of Singapore, sinking them with the loss of nearly 1,000 lives. 2,000 survivors were picked up by British destroyers.

- **NEWS: The fall of Singapore, the 'Bastion of Empire'.**

In February 1942, General Percival was forced to surrender to save further loss of civilian life. Singapore had been poorly defended; the big guns pointed out to sea, but the Japanese attacked through the Malayan peninsula. They used their bases in French Indo-China to invade the kingdom of Siam, from where they made their assault on British Malaya.

I was shushed as the family listened to the wireless. Poor old Churchill sounded very sad as he spoke about this disaster. Dad said it meant the beginning of the end for our Empire.

Disaster followed disaster as Japanese soldiers swarmed over South East Asia and Japanese ships landed troops on as many islands as they could reach, fighting to the last man. They succeeded in invading Hong Kong (British), the Dutch East Indies and the Philippines (USA).

They also attacked New Guinea and the Solomon Islands (both British), but were repelled by troops from Australia and New Zealand. They bombed Australia, launched a series of air attacks on British Ceylon (now Sri Lanka) and invaded Burma (British), where they fought all the way to India before British and Australian troops finally pushed them back again.

The next new phrase I heard from Dad was 'Second Front Now!'

Stalin sent his foreign minister Molotov to London in April 1942 to plead for Britain and the USA to mount an attack from the West – a Second Front to attract the German armies away from the Eastern Front, where they were overwhelming the Red Army and slaughtering thousands of Russian civilians.

At this time, however, British, Indian and Polish troops were fighting in the Desert War against German and Italian armies in North Africa. Other British and Australian troops were fighting the Japanese in Burma. And the Americans were fully engaged against the Japanese Navy in the Pacific Ocean.

Under continual bombardment, the Royal Navy escorted convoys across the Mediterranean to supply our troops. Some British army officers created the Long-Range Desert Force, forerunner of the SAS (Special Air Service), which made clandestine raids behind enemy lines to sabotage aircraft, tanks and so on.

- **NEWS: American troops surrender in the Philippine Islands.**

In May 1942, 60,000 American troops surrendered to the Japanese in the Philippines. General MacArthur, who had already left, made a determined promise, "I shall return."

- **NEWS: A great naval victory by the Americans in the battle of Midway.**

In June 1942, the Japanese suffered their first significant defeat by the Americans, which put an end to their further expansion in the Pacific.

But all this was above my head. I was sitting at my desk in school, writing the date at the top of the page in my exercise book when, as I carefully printed out 1942, it struck me for the first time that the years were being counted as they went by. What would it be like when the numbers reached 1950? How could they ever reach 1960? I would be *old*! My heart sank. I didn't want to grow up – it was such fun being a child.

One Sunday, Mum and Dad took me for a trip to the Cockney market in Petticoat Lane. This was only open on Sundays and I was excited to see the busy market with its shouting and bartering at a time when all the shops everywhere else were shut. Normally on Sundays there was hardly any traffic and everything was very quiet. Even the church bells were silent, because the Government had ordered them to be rung only as a warning in the case of Invasion.

Another day Mum took me out on the Green Line bus *(a green coach from London stopping at bus stops in rural areas)*. We walked along the winding country lanes, sometimes meeting the odd farm tractor or hay wagon. *There were hardly any private cars and no motorways in those days.* We enjoyed a picnic lunch in the woods and I had a lovely time exploring. Then, on our way home along the main road (the arterial road, as we called it), which ran through open farmland, we saw some men working in a field on the other side.

The men were wearing shirts with the letters POW (Prisoner of War) marked in black across the back. Mum startled me by saying, "Oh look, those are Italians, I do like Italians," and took me by the hand to cross the road to walk past them. Red-faced and hot with embarrassment, I kept my eyes down and thought, "How *could* she? What will they *think* of us?" One of the prisoners was just coming out of the gate as we passed it, carrying a sack of vegetables on his back, and he politely stood back to let us go by. My mother smiled at him and I wished there were a hole I could sink into. *(I didn't know at the time, but my mother's grandfather was Italian.)*

Summer holidays during the war years were hot and sunny and I was out with my friends nearly every day. One of our adventures was to squeeze through a gap in the railings at the end of the road and climb down to the railway track. There was a little trail through the grass and shrubs alongside the line, which we followed, pretending to be explorers in foreign lands. It got even more interesting when we came across a canal. At night I had vivid dreams, usually along the lines of sailing a boat down the river to the sea and off to a faraway land – a cross between 'The Wind in the Willows' and 'The Wizard of Oz'.

So I went my merry way, confident of being unnoticed by the grown-ups. They were otherwise occupied – and they were more interested in talking about the News than anything I was doing! Anyway, whenever I tried to have a conversation with them, they could be so annoying. Once I'd asked Nana how old she was – and she said, "17!" I was *very* suspicious. And when I'd asked Auntie Nellie *her* age (I was always curious about how old they all were) she'd said, "As old as my tongue and a little older than my teeth." Whenever I asked Dad how old *he* was, he said, "99." He was 99 during all the years I was growing up.

In August, for my 8th birthday present, I was given a second-hand 'fairy cycle' by one of the neighbours and Frank helped me learn how to ride on two wheels instead of the three which I'd had on my old tricycle. From then on, I discarded my scooter and rode my little bicycle to school every day. I always enjoyed 'helping' Frank to mend punctures in his bicycle tyres, because this meant messing around with bowls of water in the driveway and seeing air bubbles come up from the hole in the inner tube. Now, I thought, he can help me mend any punctures in my own tyres.

- *NEWS: Victory at Alamein!*

In October 1942, the British 8th Army in North Africa, led by General Montgomery, finally won victory at El Alamein over the famous German General Rommel, known as the Desert Fox.

This was our first major success since our victory in the Battle of Britain and everyone was delighted. With the family listening to the wireless, I heard Churchill saying, "It is not the End. It is not even the Beginning of the End. But it is, perhaps, the End of the Beginning."

In November 1942 American troops were brought over the Atlantic to help finish the Desert War, landing in North West Africa to fight French Vichy troops, but they suffered unexpected battle losses before recovering the situation.

In December 1942 British destroyers, on convoy escort duty on the Murmansk run, outfought both a battleship and a heavy cruiser from a German Navy task force. This enraged Hitler so much that he ordered the task force to be scrapped so that the guns could be used on land. From that time the German surface fleet played no significant part in the war.

Now at night the noise of hundreds of planes flying overhead meant that *our* bombers were on the way to Germany. Dad told me the RAF flew their Lancaster bombers in 'streams' – on occasion as many as 1000 aircraft in one night. Often, lying in bed, I could hear the steady roar of the engines, quite a different sound to the heavy, uneven grumbling of the German bombers.

I knew that the Americans had joined in the bombing of Germany, but they preferred to operate during daylight and flew in heavily armed Flying Fortresses (B.17s) in close formation for mutual defence.

Unlike German bombers who only needed to hop across the Channel to bomb British cities, Allied bombers were compelled to fly a much longer distance across occupied territories, through the flak from German anti-aircraft guns both on the way there and coming back. Many bomber crews, flying during the hours of darkness, were caught in searchlights and shot down. Approximately 55,000 British airmen lost their lives, but others managed to fly their damaged planes back to England.

We heard a new song on the wireless: 'Coming Home on a Wing and a Prayer . . .'

Factories in Britain worked round the clock to keep the RAF supplied with new and better aircraft.

Then another new phrase cropped up in people's conversation: 'Tip-and-Run raid'.

The Germans retaliated to the Allies' bombing with daytime attacks on our historic towns and cities. People called them Tip-and-Run raids but they were more properly known as the Baedeker raids, since the targets were selected from the famous pre-war Baedeker guidebooks, which listed places of historical interest over Europe and the British Isles.

The enemy bombed cities valued as our heritage, for example York, Canterbury, Norwich, etc., although none of course had any military significance. Baedeker raids continued through 1942 until early 1943.

11. Yankee Doodle Dandy ~ 1943/44

On the wireless we heard a lot of American songs: 'Over There'; 'This is the Army, Mr Jones'; 'Don't go Walking down Lover's Lane with Anyone Else but Me'; 'Don't Fence Me In'; 'Deep in the Heart of Texas'. And Glenn Miller's band was becoming famous.

On a visit to the West End with Mum, I saw American GIs *(GI stood for General Issue)* crowding the streets. Their uniforms were smarter and more attractive than those of our own 'Tommies' and the sound of their voices had the glamour of the Hollywood film stars.

I heard that our Tommies were rather bemused. GIs were much better paid, had unlimited supplies and generously splashed their money around, so that an English girl was delighted to have an American boyfriend, especially when he gave her presents of nylon stockings, previously unheard of, or a box of chocolates, impossible to find in English shops. And there were a lot of wartime romances. I imagined that blacked-out and battered London was an exciting place for romance, especially when the nightingale sang in Berkeley Square . . .

An unkind joke went around: "Overpaid, Overfed, Oversexed and Over *Here!*" Our soldiers also disapproved of the Americans' attitude towards their black compatriots, who were not permitted to eat or drink with white Americans or to attend the social events and dances they arranged for meeting local people.

On the other hand, many English families welcomed the Americans into their homes. Once Barbara invited a couple of them to supper to see how an English family lived and we were bowled over by their easy-going friendliness and informality.

At this time Barbara and Truda were both finishing a course at the same secretarial college while my sister was waiting to be 'called up' but out of the blue Barbara announced that she'd made up her mind to volunteer, so that she wouldn't be sent to work somewhere she didn't like.

Our cousins (three sons of one of Dad's elder brothers) were all in the armed forces – the youngest, John, used to be Barbara's childhood playmate and he had joined the RAF. Barbara chose the Wrens (Women's Royal Naval Service). Apart from military service, the only other options for young women when they were called up were to work in factories making munitions or aircraft, or to join the Land Army and work on the farms.

Truda didn't know yet what work she would do. As a German she was not permitted to join the military services. In any case, as a Quaker, she was a pacifist.

Barbara was posted to Scapa Flow, the Royal Navy base in the Orkney Islands, where she was put on a training course in aircraft maintenance for the Fleet Air Arm. When she had gone, I heard the family talking about a German U-boat, which had daringly crept into Scapa Flow undetected at the beginning of the war and had torpedoed and sunk the famous HMS Royal Oak, with the loss of hundreds of British sailors' lives.

Barbara told us in a letter that the crossing from Scotland to the Orkney Islands over the Pentland Firth was a very rough trip. She also told us that among all the shipping in Scapa Flow there were several aircraft carriers; and the aircraft from these arrived regularly for maintenance at the airfield where she was being trained. In the camp there were classical record concerts on Sundays and one evening the famous violinist Yehudi Menuhin came to play. Barbara made lots of friends, including several local Orkney people.

I missed my big sister. She was away for months at a time. Having Truda there was just not the same. It was a lovely surprise to come in from school one day and find Barbara home on leave. I was always pleased when the whole family was together and Barbara kept us all in fits of laughter with stories of life in the Wrens.

One of the stories Barbara told us was that she'd gone out in the evening with a sailor boyfriend and was very late getting back to barracks. It was dark and she was locked out! To avoid awkward questions she climbed through an open window, but as she jumped down inside she fell into the arms of a naval officer, who raised his eyebrows and said, "My dear Wren, do you make a habit of coming in by this method?"

Barbara said that her worst moment in the Wrens was when she had to climb the rope ladder up the side of an enormous ship. The best moment was realizing she was the only girl on board!

Eventually Barbara started bringing home her current boyfriend when she was on leave. There were several boyfriends over the years, all in the armed services.

Once Barbara brought home a bomber pilot who stayed late in the evening because an air-raid had started. Although the first main Blitz was over, there were still intermittent air raids, but we were no longer in the habit of rushing to the shelter every time the siren went off. Barbara's pilot boyfriend couldn't understand why we were carrying on as usual. Mum glanced across the room and saw that he was very pale. "What's the matter with you? You're a Bomber Pilot, for goodness sake!" He said, "Yes, but down here you're just Sitting Ducks! I'd feel a lot safer up there, flying." We all hastened to assure him he was in a 'Safe Area' and we would take cover if the bombs got any nearer.

On another occasion I was most impressed by a magnificent Scottish Highlander who turned up one day in full dress uniform with kilt. He was very tall – towering over my sister, who was particularly tall.

Then one day Barbara brought home a handsome Dutch sailor, who joined in with a family game of Monopoly and kept us entertained with a stream of funny stories. At nearly nine years old I was so taken with him I asked him, "If you're not going to marry Barbara, would you marry me?" This caused much embarrassment to Barbara and merriment all round. I felt my cheeks getting hot and tried to explain that I meant this for when I grew up. But they just went on laughing . . .

- *NEWS: Allied landings in Sicily.*

Following the Allied invasion of Sicily in July 1943, German troops put up fierce resistance as the British 8th Army fought its way up one side of the leg of Italy while the American 5th Army fought its way up the other side. Most of the Italians were happy to change sides and their Fascist leader Mussolini fled.

Mussolini was later captured at the end of the war, along with his mistress, by the Partisans (Italian freedom fighters) who shot both of them and strung up their bodies upside down in a public square. The Pope intervened, pleading for them to be taken down and given a decent burial.

On my 9th birthday Truda came home from work with a special present for me. She placed a very large orange on my plate, the first I'd seen since early in the war. I didn't like to ask her, but I guessed an American boyfriend had given it to her.

By the end of 1943 the number of American troops arriving in England had grown to thousands. They were brought over in the British transatlantic liners, Queen Mary and Queen Elizabeth, as there were no other ships large enough to carry sufficient troops, or fast enough to outrun the German U-boats. The merchant convoys were too slow and subject to attack.

We went to see a stage musical in which the American star Mickey Rooney sang, 'I'm a Yankee Doodle Dandy'. Dad and I thought this was a great song and liked singing it around the house at the top of our voices . . . until Mum's patience ran out.

For quite some while I had got into the habit of borrowing books from the junior section of Enfield Town Library. This was, for me, a favourite place to call in on my way home from school. I hunted out adventure books every week, carrying them, three or four at a time, home across the park and up the lane in eager anticipation of a good read. There were notices all around the library – SILENCE – but people talked in whispers! *There were only hard-cover books in libraries – no paperbacks, computers, CDs or DVDs in those days.*

When I'd first been introduced to the library I was only interested in adventure books by Enid Blyton, but by this time I was reading other writers, such as Arthur Ransome, Alison Uttley and Malcolm Saville. The grown-ups called me a 'bookworm'.

I particularly enjoyed adventures with Worrals. The famous author Captain Johns, who wrote a series of books for boys about Biggles, the intrepid flyer, also wrote another series for girls, featuring Worrals, the brave WAAF pilot. Worrals got mixed up in all kinds of daring wartime exploits abroad. She had no time for male chauvinism and got very annoyed with senior male officers who were inclined to express doubts when she proposed flying off in her beloved Spitfire to sabotage enemy assets or rescue British prisoners. *(I think Worrals was an early modern feminist!)*

I also enjoyed all the stories by Richmal Crompton about 11-year-old William. When my mother was not well for a while, lying on a mattress on the floor next to the Morrison shelter, I read aloud to her the one about William discovering there were such things as begging letters, thinking these were a jolly good way of getting hold of some money and writing one to someone he thought was very rich. He wrote what, in his opinion, was a heartrending letter, terribly exaggerated and full of spelling mistakes, about all the imaginary tragedies he was suffering, and Mum and I laughed so much that I had to stop reading for a fit of hiccups.

The sirens wailed more often again as the Germans stepped up their attacks on London, sending bomber planes up the Thames almost every night for several weeks. *These air raids, early in 1944, later came to be known as the Little Blitz.*

Frank told me to watch out for butterfly bombs, little explosive devices with butterfly wings, which were dropped in their thousands and were caught up in trees or hedgerows, or scattered on the ground. Children were warned not to pick them up because they were designed to explode as soon as they were disturbed.

Early in 1944, the British, helped by Chinese soldiers and supported by parachute drops of supplies from American aircraft, finally won a hard victory against the Japanese at Imphal (in a remote valley near the Himalayas) and saved India from a Japanese invasion. The American 'airlift' was protected by the RAF, who also harried the Japanese army with bombing and strafing.

By this time I was often hearing mention of D-Day. From time to time I wondered what this was, but my attention was usually elsewhere. In out-of-school hours my friends and I had more immediate things to occupy us, such as climbing the big trees that grew along the edge of the golf-links – we were able to get a good start by climbing on top of the iron railings that ran beside them – or practising hand-stands on the grass.

Months passed. All the grown-ups could talk about was D-Day. Did this mean the end of the war?

At last came the day.

- **NEWS: D-Day Landings! (6th June 1944)**

With the rest of the family listening to the wireless, I had to be quiet and listen too. Now I knew what 'D-Day' meant. This was the day the Allies landed on German-occupied territory to fight the enemy through France and into the heart of Germany. I asked Dad what the 'D' stood for and he told me, "Deliverance!"

British, Canadian and American troops had spent over a year training in military camps extending along the whole of the south coast of England, filling fields and roads with tents, trucks, tanks, guns and the rest of their equipment, in preparation for the assault on five beaches in Normandy, France.

The armed forces used code names for military operations. Operation Overlord was the code name for the Allied invasion of north-west Europe.

The assault phase of Operation Overlord was known as Operation Neptune, which involved landing the troops on the beaches and all the other associated naval and air supporting operations required to establish a beachhead in France.

On D-Day the American forces landed 73,000 troops on two of the five beaches, while in the British and Canadian sectors 83,115 troops were landed on the other three beaches, 61,715 of them British; naval personnel included 52,889 Americans and 112,824 British; airborne troops numbered 15,500 Americans and 7,900 British (statistics from the Portsmouth D-Day Museum).

Everyone at home thought the war was coming to an end. Some people said, "It will all be over by Christmas!"

I heard Dad talking about Mulberry Harbours and asked him what these were. He explained that our troops had to avoid heavily defended ports; they could only land on open beaches, but these had no harbour facilities. To solve this problem Churchill had come up with one of his bright ideas! He gave instructions to construct floating harbours and British engineers had spent months building enormous concrete caissons and wooden jetties to be towed across the Channel. These provided the required facilities for landing armoured transports, tanks, ammunition, rations and further troop reinforcements.

12. I Knew Hitler's Name But He Didn't Know Mine ~ 1944/45

We began to have second thoughts about the war being over by Christmas, when the first Flying Bomb arrived soon after D-Day. The enemy had invented a new kind of pilot-less aeroplane packed with explosives, the engine primed to stop when it reached London so that it dropped and blew up as a huge bomb. At first, everybody called them Flying Bombs; but some wit soon came up with the most fitting word – Doodlebugs! These could arrive any time, day or night. Now there were no 'safe' areas left in London. It was back to sleeping every night in the Morrison shelter.

One Saturday, on the way to call on my friends, I was opening the front garden gate when I heard a harsh engine noise like a noisy motor-bike, getting louder and louder. I stopped short when I saw a Doodlebug, just above rooftop height, coming straight down the road. Transfixed, I watched it roar past. It was like a little dirty grey plane with short stubby wings, but instead of a proper tail there was a fat pipe at the back, blowing out flames. Bits of its rough metal body glinted in the sunshine.

Mum was at the open front door screaming, "Pat! PAT!" and I shouted impatiently over my shoulder, "It's all right, it's all *right!* It's going *past!*" Didn't she know I was nearly 10 years old? I could look after myself! A minute or so later, the noise stopped abruptly. A few seconds hush . . . a distant heavy explosion.

Heavy guns, manned by the Home Guard, had been hurried down to the coast in the hope of shooting down Doodlebugs while they were still over the sea, for the British already knew of the threat from Hitler's 'secret weapon' thanks to liaison between British Intelligence and the Polish resistance movement known as the Polish Underground Army.

The Poles had managed to acquire and dismantle a Doodlebug that was being tested in their country and had landed but failed to explode. Under the nose of the enemy, a flight path was set up in open country for a plane from England, which landed under cover of darkness, waited while the parts of the Doodlebug were quickly loaded and took off again just in time before the Germans arrived to investigate.

The Home Guard managed to shoot and explode a number of Doodlebugs before they reached the coastline. Sometimes Spitfire pilots were also successful, at great risk to themselves, in catching up with them over the sea and firing to explode them – at the same time trying to dodge the worst of the blast. Some pilots even managed to fly alongside a Doodlebug, touching wingtip to wingtip until they could tip it over into the sea.

Until now, Jerry hadn't shown any interest in our little road, but it seemed to me that he was sending all the Doodlebugs our way. One evening after dark when we heard one coming very close, we all hurried to crouch inside the Morrison shelter. The noise got louder and louder until, just at the point when it sounded as though it was right above our roof, it *stopped!* Deathly silence . . . I squeezed my eyes tight shut, Mum gripped my hand and nobody said a word.

Then Frank shifted, knocking his head on the iron ceiling of the shelter – BOOM! My deaf Dad heaved a sigh of relief and muttered, "My God, that was a close one," and Mum, Frank and I collapsed into a heap of hysterical giggles. Meanwhile, thank God, the Doodlebug's momentum carried it on until it crashed, somewhere beyond the railway cutting which passed by the end of the road.

Dad thought it would be a good idea to get away for a holiday. It was difficult to get a train because they were often earmarked for carrying troops, or the railway lines were still in disrepair after bombing. And then there were the posters on every station asking, 'Is Your Journey Really Necessary?'

The whole strip of land and beaches along the south coast was out of bounds, taken over by the military, so Dad chose North Devon. He made a booking for the family (except for Barbara, who was still in the Orkney Islands) at a bed-and-breakfast house from Saturday to Saturday.

It was impossible to get a train on that Saturday morning, so Dad proposed we travel on Friday and sleep on the beach overnight. I was delighted to find our train had a corridor. This meant we would go fast, non-stop, for a long distance. I spent a lot of the journey staggering along the swaying corridor or leaning out of the window risking smuts in my eyes. As we got nearer to Devon, I was thrilled when I caught my first glimpse of the sea between two hills. At last the journey came to an end and Dad, as was his habit, along with a few other people, went up the platform to thank the train-driver for a safe journey.

We spent the night uncomfortably in deck-chairs on the beach at Ilfracombe. I don't think any of us got much sleep. We had to take shelter in a cave while a storm passed over! By 6 o'clock next morning Mum and Dad were dying for a cup of tea and decided it was time to start the day. We stacked up the deck chairs and climbed up to the promenade. At the top of the steps there was a large notice board facing the street and we turned around to read it. The message was stark: ANYONE FOUND ON THE BEACH AFTER MIDNIGHT IS LIABLE TO BE SHOT ON SIGHT.

Here in peaceful Devon, this came as a shock! Mum, Frank and I all looked round fearfully to see if anyone had noticed us, but Dad laughed it off. He said the local people probably hadn't bothered to take the notice down when the threat of invasion had passed. Thank goodness nobody was about, I thought. They might have been a bit suspicious to see a group of strangers coming off the beach at that time in the morning. We hurried away to find an early-opening café for breakfast.

Later we took the bus to Combe Martin, where we were going to stay. From the moment I glimpsed, from the top of the bus, the little harbour between two steep hills, that holiday was bliss. No sirens, no doodlebugs. It was as though the war belonged to another world.

We went swimming off the rocks and explored the caves. We spent days walking over hills or through valleys by chattering streams, where I was enchanted with the myriads of tiny waterfalls over the rocks and wanted to paddle or jump from rock to rock, teetering on the edge of falling in. We stopped at any farm we came across for refreshments. A huge barrel of fresh frothy milk with a tap was always available to fill a mug, free of charge.

One day we climbed to the top of the steep hill known as Little Hangman, overlooking Combe Martin harbour. Another higher hill nearby was called Big Hangman. There were wonderful views from the top along the rocky coastline.

Another day we walked several miles and found the beautiful Hunter's Inn, set in a deep valley with a wide rocky stream flowing down to the sea through the woods. The hill-tops above the treeline were covered in heather. We were told by the local people that this place was known as Little Switzerland. After following the stream down through the woods to the little cove for a swim, we made our way back, with several interruptions for me to cross the stream, either balancing on a handy log, or using rocks as stepping stones.

Back at Hunter's Inn I was introduced to a wonderful new treat: Cream Tea with hot scones and strawberry jam. No butter, but a tumbler full of clotted cream! Then we had to walk several miles back to Combe Martin.

At the end of each day we called into the fish and chip shop down by the quay and, absolutely tired out, walked slowly in the darkness up the village street to our lodgings, while we ate the food, liberally sprinkled with salt and vinegar, out of newspapers. Fish and chips have never tasted so good since that time!

In Devon, instead of removing or blanking out the signposts, the local people had just turned them to face in the wrong direction. Every time we set off to find a particular place we would come to a turning in the lane where there was a signpost stating the name of the place and the distance – 3 miles – and pointing back the way we had come. No matter how far or in which direction we walked, when we came to a signpost, the place we were looking for was always back where we had come from – and the distance was always 3 miles!

Dad took my mind off the frustration by making me laugh at the thought of mighty Panzer tanks rumbling down our little Devonshire country lanes with the enemy soldiers scratching their heads, confused, lost and quite defeated by this brilliant idea of the locals!

When we got home Doodlebugs were still coming over every day, but they were usually far enough away to watch as they rattled past high in the sky. Everybody looked up when they heard the peculiar, rough noise of the engine to see which way it was headed, but if it was high up and passing by there was no need to dive for cover. You just stood and watched. When the noise of the engine stopped, seconds passed slowly in silence. Then – a distant heavy explosion.

In all, 2,400 Doodlebugs crashed on London over the period between June 1944 and March 1945. Enfield was hit by 20. They killed another 5,000 Londoners and caused immense damage.

At least people could see or hear the Doodlebugs coming, but Jerry's next secret weapon was even more deadly. The Rockets or V2s (Doodlebugs were more properly called V1s) came across faster than sound. Devastating explosions took place day or night without warning and people were killed outright. What use were sirens now?

The neighbours all said, "If it's got your name on it there's nothing you can do – but if it hasn't, there's no need to worry." I didn't find this much comfort! I tried cheering myself up with the thought that I knew Hitler's name but he didn't know mine. But at 10 years old I had a strong suspicion that the neighbours were just blustering.

The V2 was a supersonic rocket, which flew up to 60 miles high in an arc to fall on London without warning. German scientists had been developing rocket propulsion from the beginning of the war. The British knew what they were doing, but RAF Bomber Command was unable to locate and destroy the mobile launching sites. Now the British army was on the way to find them.

In all, 517 rockets hit London between September 1944 and March 1945, ten on Enfield, killing another 2,600 Londoners.

These 'Vengeance' weapons were so called, Dad told me, because the Germans were outraged by Allied air raids on German cities and civilians. It was *my* turn to be outraged. What about *their* air raids on *our* cities and civilians? What about *our* vengeance? Did they think they could just bomb and invade other people's countries all over Europe without any comeback? Anyway, didn't Bomber Harris promise that they will reap the Whirlwind?

Mum and Dad listened to every news bulletin. The allied forces in France were meeting fierce resistance but the search was on for the missile launchers aimed at London.

In September 1944, British forces fighting in Belgium reached and liberated the capital city of Brussels. That same month German forces surrendered to the Americans in Luxembourg.

Surely the war was coming to an end. Everyone was sick and tired of it, but still the Germans carried on fighting.

I heard talk of two terrible air-raids which the British and Americans carried out on Dresden in Germany, leaving it in rubble and flames.

These raids caused a firestorm in the city centre, killing approximately 40,000 civilians. They were controversial then and have been so ever since, but at that time, in February 1945, they were in response to an urgent appeal by the Russians, for Dresden was a railroad junction delivering train-loads of German troops to fight against the Red Army. There were also four big armaments factories in the city. The bombers, however, inadvertently did more damage to the city centre than to military targets.

In justification, it was argued that the raids were carried out in the face of Hitler's aggressive 'Total War' (and the brutality against civilians by invading German troops) and his stubborn refusal to surrender, bringing ever more death across Europe.

- **NEWS: Death of President Roosevelt (12th April 1945)**

Shock and dismay all round. Everyone knew that Roosevelt had suffered poor health for a long time, but it seemed particularly tragic that the President of our main Ally should die just when victory was at last in sight.

Then we heard on the News that British and Canadian troops were fighting their way north to liberate Holland and Denmark from occupation on their way to north-west Germany.

In the last stages of the war, the Dutch under occupation were close to death by starvation. The RAF signalled the enemy a request to allow our Lancaster bombers to fly over Holland and drop supplies. The Germans would not promise to withhold their anti-aircraft fire, but in the event they did so and many Dutch lives were saved. This operation continued from 29th April until 8th May (BBC television documentary 2005).

- **NEWS: American and Russian forces meet at the Elbe in Germany.**

On 29th April 1945, American troops reached the western bank of the River Elbe and met up with the Russians arriving on the other side to *have a triumphant celebration. The Russians let their hair down and broke into Cossack dances.*

The British 2nd Army had also reached the Elbe further north.

- *NEWS: Russians storm Berlin!*

My Dad thought the Russians deserved to be the first to make a victorious entry into Berlin because, he said, they had sacrificed so many millions of lives. Without their vast Red Army, it would have been much harder for the British and Americans to defeat Germany's military might.

- *NEWS: Germany announces Hitler is dead!*

On 30th April 1945 the Russians found what they later guessed to be Hitler's remains – recently burnt bones – just outside his bunker. On 1st May German radio announced that Hitler had died a hero, 'fighting to the last breath.'

It was later discovered that Hitler married his mistress Eva Braun when the Russians reached the outskirts of Berlin and they committed suicide together on their wedding night, Hitler leaving instructions for their bodies to be burnt immediately. Russian troops reached the bunker about half an hour after the cremation.

13. Where Were the Bluebirds? ~ 1945

- *NEWS: German forces surrender to General Montgomery.*

On 4th May 1945, German military commanders in Holland, Denmark and north-west Germany signed surrender documents in a tent erected for the purpose near General Montgomery's HQ at Lunerberg, Germany.

Every year since the war, the Danish people have put candles in the windows of their homes on the anniversary of the day of the British liberation. Also, every year since the war, the Norwegian Government has sent over a giant Christmas Tree to London for Trafalgar Square in appreciation of the British war effort.

- *NEWS: Unconditional surrender of all German forces!*

On the 7th May, American and British commanders witnessed the signing of surrender documents by German commanders at General Eisenhower's HQ in Rheims, France, but the Russians insisted that the announcement of Victory should be delayed for another day until the Germans had surrendered formally to them.

The designer of the V2 rockets, Von Braun, made sure he surrendered to the Americans rather than the outraged British. He added insult to injury with the comment, "I aimed for the stars, but sometimes I hit London!" He was flown immediately to the USA, together with 60 large crates of technical drawings, calculations, etc. and some of his technical staff, where he was given every facility to continue his work, later heading the development of the American space rocket programme.

According to 'The Secret War' by Brian Johnson, the Americans overlooked an agreement with the British that this information and technology should be shared equally.

- *NEWS: VE Day (Victory-in-Europe Day) will be 8th May.*

At that moment life stood still. I could hardly believe it – the War was over! What would happen now? I couldn't remember how things were before War started. Wartime was the normal way of life – rationing; queues; the wireless with the News, brass bands, comedians and romantic or funny songs; the black-out; searchlights; explosions; sleeping in the Morrison shelter. It would be a strange world without War. In particular, I wondered what the BBC newsreaders would do now. There would be no more News!

The next day Mum, Dad, Frank and I went up to the West End and I looked round with amazement. Adults behaving like excited children. Streets filled with people, shouting, laughing, singing, dancing – some even clambering up lamp posts to wave flags. Complete strangers were hugging and kissing each other. We saw a couple dancing on the roof of a taxi and, over the heads of the crowd, a bus unable to move while people surged around it.

We made our way to Buckingham Palace and pushed through the crowds to find a place where we could see the balcony and wait for the King to appear. Everybody was chanting: "WE WANT THE KING! WE WANT THE KING!"

Everyone loved the quiet, hardworking King George, who had stayed in London throughout the war and visited the bombed-out Eastenders with Queen Elizabeth *(later the Queen Mother)*; and everyone agonized along with him when he had to struggle with his terrible stammer through his Christmas broadcasts.

At last the King and Queen came out on the balcony with the two princesses, Elizabeth and Margaret. They were laughing and waving to us. They disappeared inside for a while and came out again, this time with Winston Churchill, and the crowd roared with delight.

It later transpired that Princess Elizabeth – our future Queen – and her sister Princess Margaret slipped out of the palace to mingle with the crowds and join in the dancing. Princess Elizabeth had been working as a car mechanic in the ATS.

As it got dark we struggled through the crowds to Trafalgar Square, where sailors and their girlfriends were jumping and splashing in the fountains. Binny Hale, a famous stage star, came out on a balcony and sang a popular song to the crowd: 'When the Lights Go On Again, All Over the World . . .' Then she sang another: 'I'm Going to Get Lit Up When the Lights Go On in London!'

Binny Hale was dressed in top hat and tails like a man. She took her hat off, threw it down into the crowd and shouted, "Will the gentleman who caught my hat please come up and have a drink." Behind her, through the windows, we could see people having a party. I wished we had caught the hat and could go up to join in!

We went down to the Thames to see the fireworks, a marvellous display lasting for hours and finishing with an enormous royal crown of lights floating above the river. I don't remember going home. Everyone was having a wild party.

A few days later, Dad and Mum took me up to the West End again. Dad wanted me to see the lights of London and particularly the coloured moving advertisements, which I had never seen before. We waited around Piccadilly Circus as it got dark and I watched in wonder as coloured lights sprang up and flashed, creating a dancing clown on the front of a theatre and spelling out COCA COLA above a restaurant. I was full of excitement as we walked along Oxford Street. All the shop-windows were lit up, restaurant windows were lit up and even the buses had lights inside them – and their headlights were full on, without shades.

We finally went for a meal in Lyons Corner House, which was like a palace with different restaurants inside, lots of space and chandeliers, an orchestra in the main restaurant, a band in the tea-room, and so on. Lyons Corner Houses were a cut above the ordinary Lyons tea-shops where you went for a bun and a cup of tea, or perhaps a cheap meal of egg and chips.

After all this I was very conscious that we had at last 'won' the war (forgetting that Japan still had to be defeated) and that now it was Peacetime – the opposite, I thought, to Wartime. Now at last I would find out what Peacetime was like. We'd looked forward to it for so many years . . . Peacetime was going to be absolutely wonderful!

In the days following it felt really strange, if we were out after dark, to see lights everywhere: lamp-posts; traffic headlights; windows of houses where curtains were drawn back; even some shop windows lit up after closing time, which caused my mother to comment on the terrible waste of electricity and wonder how shop-owners could possibly afford it.

In Enfield Town, I was struck by the unfamiliar sight of young men out of uniform in the streets. For years, shopping with Mum, I'd only seen women, children and old people about, with occasionally a man in uniform of one kind or another, but now young men in civilian clothes were appearing everywhere, demobbed from the services. Dad told me they'd each been given a free suit, hat, shoes and a £5 note!

Another unfamiliar sight was the many rows of flat-roofed, single-storey dwellings. These were for housing people who had been 'bombed out'. Dad told me they had been pre-fabricated before erection. They soon became known by everyone as 'prefabs'. We thought they were rather ugly, but there were many people glad to live in a new little 'house', with shiny fitted kitchen and neat front garden, away from the inner cities. *Prefabs were intended to be temporary, but in many cases they were occupied for as long as 30 years.*

I had to turn my attention to the '11-plus' exam. This was the new name for the scholarship to grammar school. As my 11th birthday fell later in the year, the headmistress suggested that I should try taking the exam that term, so that I would have the chance of starting my secondary education at the grammar school in September 1945, a week after my birthday.

I knew how important it was to Mum that I passed this exam. She did not have much of an education herself because, as the eldest, she was kept home from school to help look after several younger stepbrothers and sisters (my Nana married three times!), and the most important thing for my Mum was to see her own children get a good education.

The headmistress told me I could stay at the elementary school and take the 11-plus the following year instead, but I was keyed up for it now – and on tenter-hooks for weeks after I had taken it – until the results came through with the good news that I'd passed. Now I could go to the same school where my sister used to go.

Enfield County School had begun life as a private school many years previously, but became a state grammar school to provide the opportunity of a good education to anyone who could pass the entrance exam, regardless of their parents' income or background.

There was another type of state school, the 'secondary modern', where commercial, practical or vocational skills were taught alongside the most important academic subjects such as English and maths.

Frank had missed taking the scholarship at 11 years old because he suffered badly from asthma attacks during childhood, but he became top of the class at his secondary modern school and now, aged 16, he was studying for Matriculation *(a requirement for university)* at a Technical College. He'd made up his mind to become an Architect.

Frank also joined the Air Cadets, as a preliminary to compulsory National Service when he hoped to join the RAF. One Saturday, Mum, Dad and I, despite embarrassed protestations from Frank, went down to Enfield Town to catch sight of him among the other cadets as they paraded along Church Street.

In July 1945 the General Election took place and brought in a new Labour Government under Prime Minister Clement Attlee (who had served in Churchill's War Cabinet). Dad was pleased that Labour had been chosen to bring in and develop the new Welfare State, but I felt sorry for Churchill. Somehow it seemed ungrateful.

A colleague commiserated, but Churchill said, "You cannot blame them. They have had to put up with a great deal." In 1965, when Churchill died, he was the first and only Prime Minister to be given a State Funeral. Big Ben was silenced for the day and his coffin was carried on a barge along the River Thames. The crane-drivers in the remaining docks spontaneously lowered their cranes to 'bow' as the funeral procession passed.

In his book 'Wartime and Aftermath', Bernard Bergonzi writes:

"The new Labour Government, it was believed, would continue and make permanent the wartime spirit of classless comradeship and 'fair shares'. In fact, once in office it found itself faced with quite appalling economic difficulties, when the Americans, having captured British overseas markets during the war, abruptly cut off economic aid the moment it ended. The British economy was in ruins – literally so in some cases – after six years of total war, and though an American loan was eventually negotiated the terms were harsh."

The grown-ups were gloomy these days after listening to the BBC News and Dad was always talking about unemployment and strikes. I thought about the song that promised bluebirds over the white cliffs of Dover, love and laughter and peace ever after. We'd always had plenty of love and laughter – the way of life for civilians in wartime had been an endless source of material for jokes and hilarity – and now, at last, we had 'peace'. But everything had become so dreary . . . and where were the bluebirds?

It was all a bit of an anti-climax.

The British had fought for a longer period of time, and in more parts of the world, than any other nation, pouring all their wealth and effort, over six years, into the war. Now the country was exhausted, gold and dollar reserves all paid over or still owed to the USA, and, after the destruction wrought by bombing, what infrastructure remained was in a sad state of neglect.

It has been estimated that over 62,000 civilians across Britain lost their lives to bombs, doodlebugs or rockets (including 43,000 during the first London Blitz), with 87,000 injured and two million homes destroyed (statistics from internet sources).

London, which had been the largest concentration of people ever recorded in history as living in a single community (in 1931 the density was 7,325 people to the square mile, the highest ever known), now stood with large areas of waste ground in the heart and suburbs of the city and a greatly reduced population. Many people who left at the start of the war never came back. Dense inner-city housing, factories, railways, dockyards, gas-works and water-works had all been bombed out of existence.

The great Port of London, to which merchant ships had come from all over the world, was devastated, its docks, wharves, warehouses all gone. It never regained its former position in the world and the Rotterdam docks in Holland later took the work over as container shipping replaced the old merchant vessels.

Across Europe millions of Displaced Persons and wandering and starving refugees were trying to find their way back to their homelands. It was only due to a vast humanitarian effort by the Americans that disaster was avoided

---

- *NEWS: VJ Day. Victory-in-Japan Day, 15th August 1945.*

This time we didn't have so much enthusiasm for joining in the celebrations. The Americans had dropped two new 'atom' bombs *(developed by British and American scientists)* on the Japanese islands and surrender had followed a week later. 'The Bomb' became a new topic of daily conversation and from that time everyday life somehow lost its homely optimism. The war might be over, but now the world faced a new and hideous threat – and it seemed there was no going back

As far as I could understand from family conversation, there was some hope in the formation of a new organization to keep the peace. It was called the United Nations, replacing the old League of Nations that had been set up, Dad told me, after the First World War.

In 1945, 51 nations signed a Charter of the United Nations with the intention of securing world peace. The first discussions about this had taken place between Roosevelt and Churchill during their meeting in 1941, which produced the Atlantic Charter.

14. Aftermath ~ 1945

For the first time since I could remember, a circus arrived in Enfield Town Park. I hurried down there to hang around the caravans and watch all that was going on. After a while I was invited to help with the horses, holding them by the reins between exercises or fetching buckets of drinking water from the taps in the pavilion building nearby.

Then, after pretending I knew all about horses, I was offered the chance to ride and found myself in an awkward position. At nearly 11 years old, looking much taller than my age, my pride stopped me from confessing that I'd never ridden horseback before. Luckily for me the horse, Prince, behaved like a real Gentleman. While I clung apprehensively to the front of the saddle (very conscious that I mustn't hurt his mouth by hanging on to the reins), he cantered gently across the park as far as the river, then turned and walked sedately back.

The circus people tactfully ignored my blushes of humiliation and invited me into one of their caravans to have tea. Time sped by with my new friends until it got dark and I hastened home, but it was too late. I met a very angry Dad coming down the dark lane through the golf-links on his way to find me.

When the circus left I had time on my hands. I climbed on top of the old grass-covered air raid shelter and spent long hours in the sunshine reading, or day-dreaming about running away to join a circus so that I could ride horses. One book which I'd found in the library and particularly enjoyed was 'The Circus is Coming!' by Noel Streatfield.

Mum asked Dad to take me out for the occasional day in London, as we had no plans for a holiday that year. Dad loved London and enjoyed showing me around and telling me different bits of history. The dome of St. Paul's Cathedral still dominated the skyline, but there was bomb damage everywhere and we had to pick our way across broken pavements and step round heaps of rubble.

We visited St. Paul's, still intact but standing alone in an area completely flattened by bombing. Once inside, we climbed the steps up to the Whispering Gallery, where Dad showed me how we could hear each other whispering into the wall from opposite sides of the great Dome.

Dad told me that Churchill had sent out a special order during the Blitz – "Save St Paul's, at all costs!" For Londoners at that time, St. Paul's was a symbol of defiance. A special Watch Team lived in the cathedral to deal with incendiaries the moment they fell. On one occasion the streets had to be cleared of people and rubble, while a team of bomb disposal officers risked their lives for as long as the two days it took them to dig out a huge unexploded bomb, which was buried under the cathedral precinct. They carried it carefully away on a lorry, in a special convoy of vehicles through the cleared streets, as far as Hackney Marshes where it was finally detonated.

In the City we climbed hundreds of stone steps to the top of the Monument, which was still standing in the midst of an area of bomb damage, to see the view over London.

Dad showed me how the different trades and professions were each gathered into their own corner of London: stockbrokers, banks and insurance companies in the square mile called the 'City' where I saw numerous huge bomb craters fenced off; newspaper offices along Fleet Street, which was reduced to broken buildings and pavements and uncleared rubble; solicitors in Chancery Lane and barristers nearby in Lincolns Inn and Grays Inn; doctors in Harley Street; tailors in Savile Row; and the big retail stores along Oxford Street, where bombs had left huge gaps between the buildings.

On another day out Dad took me to Trafalgar Square, where we bought peanuts in a paper bag (from the peanut-seller who was always there) and fed the pigeons thronging around our feet and flying up to perch on my outstretched arms.

Then Dad said he was going to take me for a five-mile 'country walk' in the middle of London! We walked across all the parks – the 'lungs' of London, as Dad called them. He also told me that the plane trees along London streets were the best type of tree for such a city because their leaves were so good for absorbing pollution.

As we passed by Marble Arch, Dad showed me Speakers' Corner where, he said, anyone and everyone was free to stand upon an upturned crate and speak about any subject he chose, to anyone who cared to stop and listen. This place was a platform for those who thought they knew how to put the world to rights. I saw a small crowd gathered around one speaker, who was shouting and waving his hands about. Some listened but others jeered at him, or laughed, and there were quite a few voices raised in argument.

The owner of our house, who lived across the road and was a good friend and frequent visitor, had recently been talking to Dad about mortgages. In the end, he and Dad agreed on a price and the house became our own property. After that, whenever he came to visit, the standing joke was for him to shake his head ruefully and talk about how Dad had done him down on the price of the house, which made my Dad very pleased with himself!

Truda left us to get married – she and Mum promising to keep in touch. *(Truda was so grateful to my mother for giving her a home that, 40 years later, she turned up at Mum's funeral.)*

Barbara was demobbed and got a secretarial job at the BBC. She came home most days with anecdotes to make us laugh about the flamboyant characters she met at work. She and her friend Susan, who lived across the road, often went out at weekends with their boyfriends in a foursome. Nylon stockings were in short supply and I looked on with interest when they applied Camp coffee, the cheapest available, to their bare legs and drew dark lines to represent seams down the back.

There were no more wartime anecdotes or jokes. I wanted new interests and decided I would like music lessons. Mum and Frank could both play the piano 'by ear' and often in the summer evenings, through the open window, I could hear my friend Anne down the road playing wonderful piano music. I yearned to do the same. A kindly neighbour offered to teach me without charge and I went across the road to have weekly lessons until, finally, Dad was persuaded to pay for a proper teacher, who began coaching me for the Royal College of Music examinations.

Our neighbour next door took me to see 'National Velvet' at the cinema. This was the film in which Elizabeth Taylor was given her first starring role as a young girl who trained and rode a horse in the Grand National.

After seeing this film – promoted on cinema posters as being 'In Glorious Technicolour' – my longing for a horse of my own (which had grown ever stronger when I'd read several children's library books about young girls with ponies) became almost unbearable, but I could see no way of realizing my dream. At least, I thought, I could learn to ride. I tried to persuade Mum to let me go to a riding school, but this was firmly refused. "Only the rich go riding!" Undaunted, I resolved to save my pocket money until I could buy a pair of jodhpurs which I'd seen in a saddler's shop in the high street, price £3.3s *(three guineas)*, and coveted ever since.

Barbara's boss at the BBC was Geoffrey Ely, a well-known broadcaster on farming methods. He invited her to bring me along for a weekend at his farm in Essex. I helped feed the chickens scratching about in the farmyard and explored the huge barn with a ladder leading up to the hayloft. I spent a little time watching the cows trooping into the cowshed to be milked and a much longer time lying in the sun against a haystack. Thinking of the farm in Cuffley, I wondered what shire horses did these days, for they had long since been replaced by motorised tractors.

Back home, after an exciting dash with Mum around the shops to buy all I needed in the way of school uniform and equipment – and with much grumbling from Mum about prices – I finally became a new pupil at Enfield County School in September 1945. We all felt quite strange in our uniforms of dark green gym-slips and white shirts and ties, but the headmistress told us that school uniforms made everybody equally well-dressed regardless of our parents' different incomes, thus discouraging any possible snobbery.

After assembly at the main school, the first-year classes had to walk along a lane past the playing fields to get to a separate junior school. Here, at playtime, we discovered the shell of a plane in the grounds outside, under a group of big trees. It had the number 109 painted on the fuselage and black crosses on the wings so we knew it must be a German Messerschmidt 109 shot down during the Battle of Britain. We started right away to make the most of this discovery, climbing up to stand on the wings. or swinging on a hanging piece of fuselage, which eventually broke off. The engine had been taken out but the propeller could still be moved with a bit of effort.

The first aim of the grammar school was to teach us to express our ideas in writing in straightforward grammatical English and to speak clearly so that everyone could understand. With girls from so many different backgrounds we were all given elocution lessons in our first year. *(In those days all the girls at our school were native English.)*

As a Victory treat that first term, the whole school (about 500 girls) was taken to the cinema to see 'Pimpernel Smith', with Leslie Howard as a British secret agent in France, helping to get crashed airmen back home to England. We were told by our teachers that the name 'Pimpernel' referred to the famous fictional Englishman in Baroness Orzcy's story, 'The Scarlet Pimpernel', who slipped clandestinely into France to rescue aristocratic families from the guillotine during the French revolution.

I was still in the habit of listening to family conversation and these days it was all about the Nuremberg trials. Nuremberg *(the town in Germany where Hitler had held his pre-war rallies)* was where the top Nazi leaders were being put on trial for their crimes.

The Nuremberg trials began in the autumn of 1945. The Germans had broken the currently understood 'rules of war' by attacking civilians, but 'war crimes' and 'crimes against humanity' were new concepts, arising from the horrors perpetrated by the Germans in the occupied territories.

The greatest horror was the systematic wholesale murder in gas chambers of approximately six million Jews, mostly from Poland, but including Russians, French, Belgians, Dutch, Czechoslovakians, Yugoslavians, Hungarians, Italians and Greeks.

The Allies were determined to punish those responsible. Hitler, Himmler (in charge of the death camps) and Goebbels (propaganda minister) had all committed suicide as the war ended, but there remained other German leaders to be put on trial. Goering (Chief of the Luftwaffe), among others, was sentenced to death but committed suicide the night before he was due to be executed.

15. The Beginning of the Cold War ~ 1946

Dad still listened regularly to the News on the wireless and was always talking about the difficulties the Russians were making in Berlin. I couldn't understand this. The Russians had been our allies – why weren't they our friends?

For the task of administration and restoration of the German state and the de-Nazification process, the Allied Powers had divided Germany into four zones of administration: American, British, French and Russian. But hopes of co-operation were soon dashed; the Soviets were obstructive from the start.

The Red Army took possession of an enormous quantity of German machinery, vehicles and domestic equipment, all of which was sent back to Russia, leaving the Germans even more devastated. The Soviets refused to give up any of the territory they had captured and East Germany became incorporated into the Soviet Russian empire, while the American, British and French zones of administration were all in Western Germany.

The capital Berlin in East Germany, a wasteland of rubble after the Allied bombing, was also divided into four zones of administration and Berlin, like the whole of Germany, became divided into West and East.

This was the beginning of the Cold War.

Dad quoted Churchill's words: "From Stettin in the Baltic to Trieste in the Adriatic, an Iron Curtain has descended across Europe." I remembered that we had gone to war because Germany had invaded Poland – but now Poland was trapped behind the Iron Curtain.

> "The next war will be fought with atomic bombs, and the one after that with spears." (The Observer, 1946)

Could there be another war? We'd only just finished war with Germany and Japan and now Russia was turning out to be another threat. The thought of a new kind of war with the atom bomb was terrifying, but when I talked to Dad about it he partly reassured me. He said the scientists had only just managed to produce two atom bombs and both of these had been used on Japan to bring an end to the war and save American lives. Who would be mad enough to start an atomic war?

The Victory Parade took place in June 1946 and we went up to Auntie Louie's flat in Charing Cross Road so that we could get a good view from her window overlooking the route of the procession.

The Parade was a fine sight with marching forces from Britain, Canada, Australia, New Zealand, South Africa, India and other parts of the Empire (including the Gurkhas, who were fierce fighters and proud and loyal members of the British Army), along with the Free French and the Americans, all with their different military brass bands, drummers and flags. As well as the allied armies, there were the ATS and Women's Land Army, the Royal Navy, the Wrens, the RAF, the WAAF, the London Fire Brigade, the Home Guard, the ARP and so on. Crowds cheered them as they marched along. The whole procession must have taken about three hours to pass by.

The only allied troops not invited to take part in the Victory Parade were the Poles. The new Labour Government bowed to pressure from the Soviet President Stalin, who claimed that Poland was under Russia's sphere of influence and was 'represented' at the Moscow Victory Parade in 1945. Both the USA and Britain were wary of antagonizing our erstwhile ally, but the omission from the Parade of thousands of Poles fighting on the Allied side strengthened the feeling of 'Western betrayal' in Poland, which has lasted to this day.

I heard that the Americans were impatient to bring their 'boys' home. Some of them had married wartime girlfriends in England and I saw a cinema newsreel showing a shipload of 'GI brides' departing for the USA. They crowded the deck to wave goodbye to loved ones. I thought they must be sad for they might never see England again – America was so far away!

Frank was called up to do his National Service in the RAF and sent to a training camp near Bath. He hitchhiked home at the weekend and told us that his Sergeant's first words to him were: "Am I hurting you?" Frank, mystified, said "No." Then the sergeant shouted, "Well, I SHOULD be. I'm STANDING on your HAIR – Get it CUT!"

Frank was put on a six-months training course as a Wireless Operator/Tele Printer – 'Wop/tap' – in preparation for a posting overseas. He had to learn to type to music. He also listened to Morse Code, typing into the teleprinter for transmission through land lines.

Our Great Uncle Jack from Brixham, Devon, now a widower, came to stay for a few months holiday but ended by taking up permanent residence. He moved into Frank's old bedroom, the one with the balcony. He sold his bungalow in Brixham and I was delighted when he arrived to join the family.

I spent a lot of time talking to Uncle Jack. I told him I wanted to travel all over the world. He was very emphatic: "See your own country first. It's taken me a lifetime to go all around it and – believe me – you can't beat this country for its beauty and variety of rural landscapes. And you'll find history everywhere you go."

Once, when Uncle Jack was feeling wistful, he said to me, "You know, it takes a lifetime to learn how to live and by the time you've finished learning you're too old to live it." I felt sorry for poor old Uncle Jack – I was quite sure I knew how to live!

One interesting possession of Uncle Jack's was something he called a 'stereoscope'. It looked like a short wooden telescope with a T-shape at the end, which had a groove for standing photographs. If you put two identical photographs side by side and looked at them through the single eye-piece, you could see a wonderful three-dimensional picture! I was absolutely intrigued by this and found that Uncle Jack had lots of 'double' photographs of people and places, even though photography was a very expensive hobby.

With all that was going on that year, my parents didn't know what to do with me for the summer school holidays. They thought of Barbara's friend, another ex-Wren, Mary, who lived in Newcastle and had asked Barbara to visit her there. Mary was somehow persuaded to invite me instead. This meant a long journey on my own, so when Mum took me to the railway station she buttonholed the guard and gave him half-a-crown *(2s.6d or 30 old pence)* to look after me on the train.

It was a journey on the famous Flying Scotsman, which used to travel express non-stop to Edinburgh but now, stopping on the way, took about five hours to reach Newcastle. I felt very grown up travelling by myself. The guard came along the corridor from time to time and winked at me – this was the extent of his 'looking after' – and Mary was waiting to meet me at Newcastle station.

The family had a little dog, which Mary's brother John took for a walk every night, and I was invited to go along with him. On our walks, John wanted to talk about the differences between Northerners and Southerners. I was puzzled. Until then I hadn't known I was a Southerner. I just couldn't understand why John thought there were any differences and my feelings were rather hurt!

Still, I was happy to find that this family was in the habit of eating a lot more than mine did. Perhaps Northerners always ate more food than Southerners! Mary's mother baked several family-sized pies at a time and I enjoyed having four meals a day instead of the three we had back home. I was quite sorry when the time came to say goodbye.

By the time of my 12th birthday I was still wearing plaits. No-one was fashion-conscious and I never thought about it but one day, on the way home from music lessons, I was catcalled by some boys across the road. One of them shouted, "You'd look much better if you cut off your plaits!" Badly humiliated, I hurried home. Now I could not wait to get rid of my plaits so, after five years of growing them and measuring the length every year, I persuaded Mum, who had faithfully plaited my hair every morning before school, to cut them off.

This may have had something to do with my giving up music lessons and putting aside a tentative plan to become a famous concert pianist. I argued with my conscience that all the homework I had to do every night did not leave enough spare time for practising and anyway there didn't seem to be much hope of becoming a professional pianist, famous or otherwise. A fleeting thought did cross my mind that the world might have lost a great pianist . . . !

The best thing that autumn was that I'd saved enough money to go to the saddler's shop in triumph and buy the jodhpurs. Mum, faced with 'fait accompli', gave in and from then on Dad declared to all our visitors that I was an Expensive Item. I happily started riding lessons, one hour at 5s.0d *(60 old pence)* on Saturday mornings in the lovely Autumn sunshine.

The riding school was not far off in the 'Green Belt' around London and I cycled there to save the thrupenny *(three old pence)* bus fare. On occasion Barbara was persuaded to come with me, much to the annoyance of her current boyfriend, who wanted her to spend Saturday with him. Barbara borrowed a pair of breeches from a friend who had worked as a Land Girl.

Barbara confided in me that she had met a Polish officer, Tadek (short for Tadeusz), in Scotland, where he was stationed in a Polish military camp. Since then he had moved down south and she was going to see him in Oxford, where he and his friends were attending English language classes.

From family conversation I already knew there were thousands of Poles living for the time being in Nissen huts in old army camps across England and Scotland. By this time there were many stories about the Russians shooting anyone returning home who had been fighting with the Western Allies, or who had any connection with the West.

Under the auspices of an agreement between the Polish Government-in-Exile and the British Government, those Polish servicemen and ex-prisoners-of-war, many with their families and dependants, who were unwilling to return home to a Communist regime, formed what was called the Polish Resettlement Corps and were offered the choice of settling either in Britain or in any country belonging to the British Empire and Commonwealth. Many thousands came to live in Britain, while others chose to emigrate to the USA.

In Oxford Barbara found that Tadek's friends all wanted to go home to Poland but were doubtful of a safe return. They decided that one named Ludwig would go back to see what was happening. Barbara helped them compose a letter that he would send back to Tadek, mentioning certain members of his family, so that with this pre-arranged code Tadek would be able to judge the situation. *(No letter was ever sent back to Tadek and he never found out what happened to Ludwig.)*

Uncle Jack wanted a dog and Mum was happy to go along with the idea. We acquired a golden labrador puppy and Uncle Jack named him Doric, after the collie dog he used to own. To start with, I was enthusiastic about taking Doric for a walk before breakfast, but this didn't last long. That year was the beginning of a series of freezing cold winters. It was bad enough getting up out of a warm bed into a cold bedroom to get ready for school. Walks, even breakfast, often got missed out.

Barbara brought Tadek home at Christmas to meet Mum and Dad. When he came into the sitting room and saw the lighted Christmas Tree, his eyes filled with tears. I thought how homesick he must be and felt terribly sorry for him.

Frank also came home on leave that Christmas and told us he was being posted to Egypt. Then he was rushed off to Chase Farm Hospital (our local hospital) with a grumbling appendix. The surgeon decided on an operation to remove it, in case it gave trouble again while Frank was overseas.

After that, Frank had to report to the Air Ministry in London, who sent him back to camp. However, the camp was deserted during what was now being called the 'Big Freeze-Up' – only the sergeants were left there. Coal deliveries from Wales had stopped because the trains couldn't get through and the Government imposed a three-day working week to restrict use of power – we heard on the news that even Buckingham Palace and the Houses of Parliament had to work by candlelight. *(This lasted almost three months.)* Frank said the sergeants treated him well during this time!

Frank wrote to Mum after he had gone to Liverpool to embark on the SS Sumeria, sailing to Egypt. He told her that he had inoculations on the ship, queueing in line to pass a row of doctors with syringes. The first needle was left in his arm for the second syringe and then again for the third!

The ship passed through the Bay of Biscay in a violent storm with men falling out of their bunks at night. The bunks touched each other across the lower deck with the mess table below, some 20 feet long, covered in piles of crockery which slid down the table and smashed all over the deck. Frank was seasick. He gulped down his breakfast and then rushed up on deck for fresh air. Leaning over the rails, he saw the sea just below one minute and nothing but sky the next!

When the ship turned into the Mediterranean past Gibraltar, everything changed – calm seas, blue skies. The ship called into Malta on the way to Port Said, where they transferred to a train. Arabs were trying to sell them goods. One jumped up to the open train window and snatched a pair of glasses from someone sitting opposite Frank– he saw him running away with them.

Frank ended the journey at RAF Shallufa, an airfield about 20 miles away from Port Suez at the south end of the canal. We didn't see him again for almost two years because there was no way he could travel home on leave from overseas in those chaotic days.

Tadek came often to our house and I heard that the Polish General Anders had asked the British for help to liberate his country from the hands of Soviet Russia. There had even been a tentative suggestion that we should allow the Germans to be re-armed and turned against Russia. This idea came as a bit of a shock to me. Re-arm the wicked enemy?

After six long years of war neither Britain nor the newly freed France could contemplate starting yet another war against our erstwhile ally, the USSR. Even with the assistance of re-armed German troops (this idea was actually favoured by Churchill but dismissed out of hand by the military chiefs) it was impossible to act without the agreement and co-operation of the Americans, who were already engaged, along with the British and French, in the urgent reconstruction of Germany and showed no interest in the fate of the countries of Eastern Europe.

Churchill had long foreseen a threat from Russia. However, at the Yalta conference held by the Big Three near the end of the war, the American President Roosevelt, who thought Stalin could be trusted, held private talks with him behind Churchill's back. As the leader of a bankrupt nation, Churchill had become very much the junior partner. The conference then agreed to meet Stalin's demands for territory to protect his western borders and Churchill's views on the fate of Poland were dismissed.

Thus the countries of Eastern Europe, all 'liberated' by the Red Army, became part of Stalin's soviet empire.

Mum received another letter from Frank. He told us he slept in a 24-bed hut at RAF Shallufa. He was provided with a mosquito net and the Egyptian boy Abdul kept the hut clean. Frank relayed messages by teleprinter to the other RAF stations in the Canal zone, but when the Arabs cut out and stole lengths of cables for the copper, he was assigned to send messages by Morse code. He said the Morse code was sometimes the only means of communication, carried out by sound, lights or flags, when other methods were disabled.

16. The New World Order ~ 1947

Now in Dad's occasional speeches I heard a new phrase, 'the Truman Doctrine'.

Although Stalin had promised Churchill at the Yalta Conference during the war that he would leave Greece under British protection, communist guerillas, supported by communist Yugoslavia (under Soviet Russian influence), continued to fight government troops. Russia was also putting pressure on Turkey.

Early in 1947, the British Ambassador in Washington handed over a note from His Majesty's Government, which stated that Britain could no longer afford to support Greece and Turkey with economic and military aid against a communist takeover.

The withdrawal of the British from the East Mediterranean meant that America had to step into the breach. The new American President, Harry Truman, made a proclamation in March 1947, promising military support to Greece and Turkey to prevent them falling into Soviet hands. This became known as the Truman Doctrine.

On a visit to the cinema we saw a news documentary of Princess Elizabeth during her tour of South Africa when, on her 21st birthday in April 1947, she made a speech vowing lifelong service to the British Commonwealth. After this, there was much optimistic talk about 'the New Elizabethan Age.'

- *NEWS: Marshall Plan unveiled.*

In Western Europe, conditions still remained desperate two years after the end of the war. The Americans feared that Communism might start winning more support and could spread further west. To counter this, the American Secretary of State George Marshall called for a massive U.S. aid programme for Western Europe and what became known as the Marshall Plan was announced in June 1947.

Also in 1947 the Labour Government invited people from the British colonies in the West Indies to settle and work in England, for there was a huge shortage of labour following the loss of so many men in the war. The opportunity of earning a better living attracted many, who arrived by sea. That year the first large wave of immigrants took place and as time went on more shiploads of immigrants arrived.

It was around now that I realised we'd started dismantling our Empire, beginning with India. The British were simply packing up, handing over and departing. When I wondered why, Dad told me the colonies were demanding self-government and in any case we could no longer afford the cost of governing them.

A bankrupt Britain could not even pay the bill for the Lend Lease of aid and armaments sent by the USA *(it was to be more than 60 years before Britain finally cleared the debt)* and the Americans, who had by now captured British overseas markets, had made it quite clear they wanted to see the end of the old British Empire.

In his recently published book, 'After the Victorians', A.N. Wilson wrote:

"In terms of Britain's Victorian economic ascendancy in the world, that was on the wane by 1929, and the Finest Hour determined that Britain would be not merely economically ruined, but also politically. This might have been in the long term an inevitability. It was not an accident, if by accident one means something which comes about by mere chance or by impersonal forces. It was quite clearly decided by the US treasury and by the US State Department that if support was given to President Roosevelt's desire to help Britain and France in the war, there should be a price exacted. And that price was, and should be, the effective dismantling of Britain as a first-rank world economic power."

This meant also that the British lost their scientific pre-eminence. With reference to radar, vital in the Battle of Britain, and to nuclear research leading to the atom bomb, Wilson wrote: "... [the British] put at the disposal of the Americans every single patented and secret device which had been pioneered by British scientists and engineers. The pattern was established which came to be known as the Brain Drain, of British technological and scientific expertise being drawn inexorably towards the magnet of superior American resources."

Dad told me Churchill knew that 'he who pays the Piper calls the Tune' – 'he' in this case being the USA and the 'tune' the New World Order desired by the Americans, whose terms Churchill was obliged to accept. I felt rather sorry for Churchill. He'd always spoken of the empire – our 'family of nations' – with affection and pride and its break up must have seemed a poor reward for all his efforts and his inspiring words which had encouraged us all towards Victory.

In India, despite the efforts of Gandhi (political and spiritual leader of the Indian Independence Movement), who had worked in co-operation with the last British Governor, Lord Mountbatten, the preparations for independence provoked a bloodbath between Hindu and Moslem, which climaxed with the separation of part of India to become the Muslim state of Pakistan. This new state had two wings: the north-west and north-east of India – the eastern state eventually becoming the independent Bangladesh.

Dad declared that empires were out of date in modern times. In later years he also told me, with some pride, that our empire was the only one in history to relinquish territorial possessions without conflict. Generally the parting between the regional British Governor and the local population was friendly – the Governor had always seen his primary role as promoting the welfare and progress of the indigenous people – and the colonies all opted to remain within the British Commonwealth in order to retain their trading links.

As the remaining colonies were given their independence over the following decades, some people expressed the view that the removal of local British administrations led, in some ex-colonies, to civil wars or corrupt governments as, for example, in Africa, with the re-emergence of old-inter-tribal conflicts or growing communist influence. It has since been acknowledged that 'Pax Britannica' was a period of the most widespread stability ever known in history.

Sometimes Tadek brought along his friend Adam on a visit. Adam was very quiet and reserved. Barbara later told me he had fought in the Polish Underground Army. I never found out about Adam's experiences. I knew it was Not Done to bring up the war in conversation with anyone who had been fighting in it – unless they wanted to tell a funny story, like our cousin Clem!

Clem had fought in North Africa and once he told us how he and his fellow soldiers had come across a native sitting by a heap of stones and looking very frightened. When they asked him what the matter was, he said the witchdoctor had got very angry with him and put a curse on him. He was afraid he was going to die! No matter how hard they tried to persuade him that he would be all right, he refused to leave the heap of stones; they were some sort of protection against the curse – never mind the Desert War!

Barbara let it be known that Tadek and she wanted to get married. Mum and Dad persuaded her to take me away on holiday that year and "think about the future" to make certain this was what she really wanted. I was very happy with this idea but guessed that Barbara was not so keen. Still, Barbara agreed to a short holiday in Inverary, Scotland, where Tadek had been encamped, and we travelled by the overnight train from London to Glasgow, then on buses to the tiny town of Inverary on Loch Fyne.

After the 'Big Freeze Up' of the previous winter, Scotland was now sweltering under a heatwave. One of the first things we did was to walk along Loch Fyne as far as Tadek's old camp, which we found abandoned but with the Nissen huts still in place. Wandering around, we found a hut with notices and lists still stuck on the walls and found Tadek's name on one of the lists.

It was so hot we spent a lot of our time bathing in the loch, but we had to avoid the long, stinging tentacles of groups of jelly-fish near the shore. Sometimes we went exploring and cooled off by paddling in the peat-brown streams, which chattered over the rocks just like the Devonshire streams I'd seen on holiday at Combe Martin. Here in Scotland the colour of the water was golden-brown in sunshine, wine-red in the shade of the trees. For me it was another lovely holiday, exploring, clambering around waterfalls, rowing a boat on the loch or swimming.

Barbara introduced me to the new experience of Morning Coffee at a little café in the town and we enjoyed ourselves, making friends with a group of hikers on holiday at the same place. But sometimes I couldn't help thinking guiltily of Tadek, left sad and lonely in London waiting for Barbara to come home.

In the end, Tadek, as Barbara's future husband, was invited to live with us as part of the family while he looked for employment, but he had to sleep on the settee/put-u-up downstairs.

Tadek never spoke to us of his war experiences, but later Barbara told me that he had been taken prisoner by the Russians and had escaped from a cattle-truck train on its way to Katyn, the scene of a massacre by the Russians of 11,000 Polish officers. On his way south-west he was recaptured, this time by the Germans, but escaped again, finally making his way over the Pyrenees into Spain, where he was interned by Franco's government and later released to the British authorities in Gibraltar. The British took him to Scotland to be debriefed and that was where he and Barbara met for the first time. *(See Appendix for Tadek's full story.)*

Another letter came from Frank. He and two others had visited Port Suez "but the natives were not very friendly!" On the way back they stood on an open platform area at the end of the train, jumping off when they were near enough to walk back to Shallufa. An Egyptian policeman, who was also standing on the platform area, shouted to Frank and threw his paybook across to him. The policeman had seen an Arab lean over from the roof of the train and take the paybook from Frank's buttoned-up breast pocket – and Frank hadn't noticed anything! That policeman did Frank a good turn, for the loss of his paybook would have meant no pay and a spell in the Guardhouse – known as 'Jankers' – according to Frank.

Money was short and I had to give up riding lessons (promising myself that one day I would ride horses again) but, along with my school friends, I'd started 'going to the pictures' once a week. The price of a ticket in the stalls was only 1s.9d *(21 old pence)*. This was just about affordable out of my pocket money, which had now been increased to half-a-crown *(2s.6d or 30 old pence)*.

Many films were from Hollywood and most were in black and white. We saw 'Mrs Miniver' with Greer Garson; 'Casablanca' with Humphrey Bogart and Ingrid Bergman; and 'Yankee Doodle Dandy' with James Cagney. Johnny Weissmuller appeared in several Tarzan films. And Bob Hope teamed up with Bing Crosby and Dorothy Lamour in the first of the series of hilarious films entitled 'Road to Morocco', 'Road to Singapore', and so on.

Another memorable film was 'King Kong' *(two modern versions have since been made)*. And we were thrillingly terrified when we saw the horror film, 'The Mummy' – also when we saw Boris Karloff in one of the Frankenstein films.

One film with British actors was the tear-jerker, 'Brief Encounter', with Celia Johnson and Trevor Howard. Quite a few were British war films *(which have since become classics, portraying real historical events based on written memoirs)*.

In the auditorium, usherettes with torches walked along the aisles with big trays suspended from their shoulders, selling ice-cream, sweets and cigarettes. There was always an interlude in the middle of the programme, the lights came on and a splendid concert organ, glittering in the spotlights, rose slowly out of the floor in front of the screen, with the organist already seated and playing popular music.

At the end of the programme, which always included a 'B' film and a newsreel in addition to the main feature film, everyone stood up while the National Anthem was played.

After two or three hours of drama, adventure or romance, coming out of the cinema into the dark, quiet, half-empty street at about ten o'clock was always a comedown – something was missing and I didn't know what. Then it struck me – the trouble with Real Life was that there was no background music to match my varying moods!

It was from old newsreels repeated in the cinema that I first found out, when I was aged 13, about the death camps and what the Germans had done to the Jews. This was my introduction to horror. I'd not seen these newsreels before, because I'd only been taken by Mum to films suitable for 'family viewing'. We saw a film of the British liberation of Belsen concentration camp, where there were walking skeletons in black-and-white striped prison rags, dying people on the ground and piles of naked corpses. Another newsreel showed a film of British prisoners of war used as slave labour by the Japanese. They were so thin that their bones were sticking out.

In the postwar years there were other films depicting German atrocities against the populations of the countries they had invaded: the machine-gunning from low-flying planes of streams of fleeing refugees in France; the butchering of civilians in Russia; the mass executions and burning of villages in other occupied countries; and the use of Russian and Polish prisoners, as well as Jews, as slave labour in Germany and Poland.

We learned that there were even cases where German soldiers had shot escaping British prisoners of war – although, for the most part, the British and Americans who fell into German hands were better treated than other nationalities.

To our generation it was all a far cry from the concepts with which we'd been brought up, such as basic British decency and the old adage: 'You don't kick a man when he's already down'. Any ideas of a 'gentlemanly' war, hints of which had been shown in the Battle of Britain (when opposing pilots waggled their wings to each other to indicate they had run out of ammunition and were going home!), were now shot to pieces.

In Frank's next letter he told us that he and two others had been given five days leave and visited Cairo and the Pyramids. They saw the Sphinx, virtually buried in sand, and climbed up inside the largest Pyramid, Cheops. Then they travelled by train to Karnak and Luxor. Arabs walked the corridors calling out, "Eggs and Bread", but they were not tempted and locked the door to the corridor with the blinds down!

At Luxor they saw the Empire flying boats *(Imperial Airways)* landing on the Nile. These were a civilian version of the Sunderland flying boat, without the guns. The flying boats taxied to the shore and the passengers and crew walked across the road to stay at the riverside hotel for the night, before flying on to Khartoum and then on to South Africa.

Frank and his friends stayed at a hotel nearby where they had fresh oranges for breakfast, picked from the tree outside the dining room window! Abdul, their guide, assured them that even if they left a camera on the wall outside the hotel it would still be there in the morning. It seemed that the people there were much more honest than those in Port Said!

During that leave, Frank visited Tutankhamen's tomb, where his mummified body still lay in a beautiful, jewelled casket. The colours of the paintings on the walls, never exposed to sunlight, were still brilliant, as were the colours on the north side of the capitols of the temple columns. He also visited Queen Hatshepsut's temple at Karnak, where two massive obelisks still remained.

In November 1947, a piece of happy news was the wedding of Princess Elizabeth to Prince Philip. In those drab years after the war, this was something glamorous and exciting. Despite heavy rain, crowds of people had camped out for the whole of the previous day and night on their Blitz mattresses to make sure of saving a place on the pavements lining the route of the Bridal Procession (from Buckingham Palace to Westminster Abbey). Our family didn't do this but I did see the film footage of the wedding in a packed cinema. Princess Elizabeth had saved her clothes rationing coupons for her wedding dress of white silk. The skies cleared in time for the wedding and the bride looked radiant and beautiful.

From a school-friend I heard that I could get well-paid work – five shillings *(60 old pence)* per day – as a postman in the Christmas holidays. This meant getting up in the dark to get to the Sorting Office by 5.00 a.m., sorting letters for a couple of hours, with the help of the permanent postmen showing us temporaries how to do it, then humping the heavy sacks of mail along the streets and up the paths to each front door. There were two deliveries to make each morning – except Christmas Day when there was only one – so when the first lot had been delivered it was back to the Sorting Office to do the whole thing all over again. *(At least I didn't have to carry any junk mail – there wasn't any in those days!)*

There were compensations for all the hard work. I was always welcomed when I brought parcels and bundles of cards and often offered a half-crown tip. On Christmas morning there was sometimes even an invitation to "come in and have a drink" when people saw how much of a load I carried. But I didn't dare accept – they didn't know I was under the legal age for alcoholic drinks, because I was so tall.

Dad told me that in *his* young day he would write a letter to Mum in the morning asking her to meet him later that day; she would receive his letter in time to reply to it; and he would receive her reply in time for the meeting! There must have been at least three or four daily collections and deliveries when my parents were young.

Another thing Dad told me was that 'the Stately Homes of England' (to quote Noel Coward's song) were now being opened up to the public to bring in some money. Dad said that the aristocracy had made their homes available during the war for use by the army, the secret service or as homes for evacuees, under the principle of *noblesse oblige* – the same principle that had led their daughters to work as nurses in the mud and slaughter of the front line in the First World War. Now they needed money to refurbish and maintain the ancient buildings of Britain. *(The opening of stately homes to the public was to continue permanently.)*

17. Growing Up In A Changing World ~ 1948

My brother was due to complete his National Service in 1948, but the Israelis invaded Egypt and the Lancasters were put on alert to stop them getting near the Canal. Frank couldn't get home!

In May 1948 the new state of Israel was established, with financial help from the American Jewish population. The British administration in Palestine was no longer wanted, nor any longer willing, to control conflict between Jews and Arabs.

At the family gatherings at breakfast during weekends there was always plenty to talk about after listening to the News which, these days, always seemed to be about the threat from Soviet Russia. Everybody was taking a particular interest in Berlin.

The Soviets created an Eastern Zone currency, declared the German deutschmark illegal and made life even more difficult for the Berliners. They were also trying to rig the free elections which the Western Allies were organising.

- NEWS: Blockade of Berlin!

In June 1948 the Soviets closed all the roads, railways and waterways at the border between Western and Eastern Germany in an attempt to compel the Allies to leave Berlin. The city faced starvation. The Americans and British, both determined not to be beaten, got hold of every wartime bomber plane that could still fly and began supplying Berlin with all its needs by air from the Western Sectors, even managing to fly coal, fuel and machinery in the only planes available at the time.

The Berlin Airlift, as it eventually became known, carried on for almost a year, through the bitter German weather of the winter months in almost impossible flying conditions, sometimes with Soviet planes 'buzzing' (flying too close, circling and diving about) the unarmed Allied aircraft.

Frank finally came home on HMS 'Australia'. In England he was issued with his demob suit and carried it home in a cardboard box. Home at last! He brought a few small souvenirs as gifts. For me there was a little chiffon scarf printed with a picture of palm trees and pyramids and a necklace and pendant made with brightly coloured tiny beads. Later Frank told me that he had never wanted to do National Service, but when it was all over he was glad he had!

Uncle Jack still occupied Frank's bedroom, so I had to move out of my room to share Barbara's, while Frank moved into mine. Mum and Dad could not afford to send Frank to university, so he applied for and was given an apprenticeship with an architectural firm to gain experience while he studied at night school. He had left a girlfriend behind in England and was heartbroken because she would not wait two years and had met someone else while he was away.

Dad never missed the BBC News on the wireless and I heard him talking about 'the Malayan Emergency'.

In the complex postwar situation involving Chinese, Malays and Indians, communist guerrillas were fighting to gain the upper hand. The British had to remain in Malaya to isolate the insurgents and protect the populace until a stable government could be established. China, counted as an ally during the war, was soon to fall under the communist regime of Mao Zedong.

Also on the BBC News it was announced that the British Nationality Act of 1948 conferred the status of British Citizen on all Commonwealth subjects.

Increasing numbers of people, attracted to a life in the Mother Country, took the opportunity of coming to live in Britain. The seeds were sown for today's multi-cultural society.

One Saturday morning Tadek came up to our bedroom to waken Barbara. He bent over her bed to kiss her and at that moment I woke up myself and, feeling a bit shy, said the first thing that came into my head – "You shouldn't kiss in public!" From then on, whenever I came into a room where they were alone together, Tadek always said, "Barbara, be careful! The Public has arrived!"

The house was a bit overcrowded by this time, what with Uncle Jack and Tadek added to the family, but I loved Saturday and Sunday mornings when everybody sat around the kitchen table after breakfast, talking, arguing, laughing and drinking coffee, while Mum was busy cooking the dinner. When Tadek, in broken English, tried to explain how to cook Polish dishes, Mum's mystification caused further merriment.

Poor Tadek! We were always pulling his leg about the mistakes he made in English. He had a habit of getting everything back to front – for example, 'office-post' and 'box-letter'. He also liked what he called the 'never-forget-me' flowers *(forget-me-nots)* in the front garden. At Christmas he refused to try Mum's homemade mince pies. We couldn't understand this until we worked out that he thought they were made with minced beef filling – no wonder he didn't want to eat them with Christmas Pudding and custard!

Schooldays continued. Inside the school building we had a science laboratory, an art-room, and a library in addition to the classrooms; and the large assembly hall, also used as a gymnasium, was transformed into a theatre for school plays and for Speech Day.

Behind the school was a netball court and beyond this were two long parallel grassy mounds which were the old air-raid shelters, still in place at the edge of the playing fields, on the other side of which there were tennis courts. In autumn and spring terms we played netball and hockey, in summer term tennis and rounders, with a weekly swimming lesson at the big public open-air swimming pool not far away.

Our teachers were all middle-aged spinsters *(presumably having lost their options to marry following the deaths of so many young men in World War I)* and the general ethos of the school was the 'pursuit of excellence'.

All subjects were compulsory up to the fifth form: English and English Literature, French and French literature, History, Geography, Maths, General Science, Religious Instruction, Music, Art and P.T. In addition you could either take Classics (Latin and/or Ancient Greek) or an extra modern language, either German or Spanish. My choice was Spanish. I didn't want to learn German – old perceptions died hard!

We had a very enthusiastic English teacher whose great love was Shakespeare. Each year we studied a Shakespeare play in depth and were auditioned, selected and rehearsed to perform in the end-of-year play in front of an audience of parents and relatives. Male parts were, of course, taken by girls and, as the tallest in class, I was always pushed into auditioning for a male role – once I played Lysander in 'A Midsummer Night's Dream'.

Our teacher told us that our language had its roots in Greek, Latin and Norse, with many words adopted from other languages during the course of our explorations. She said that English was the richest and most expressive language of all. Filled with idioms and unusual turns of phrase, it continually evolved with new expressions and, spoken internationally, remained our legacy to the world.

We read Shakespeare's words:

> *This royal throne of kings, this sceptre'd isle,*
> *This earth of majesty, this seat of Mars,*
> *This other Eden, demi-Paradise;*
> *This fortress built by Nature for herself*
> *Against infection and the hand of war;*
> *This happy breed of men, this little world;*
> *This precious stone set in the silver sea,*
> *Which serves it in the office of a wall,*
> *Or as a moat defensive to a house,*
> *Against the envy of less happier lands;*
> *This blessed plot, this earth, this realm, this England.*

And a poem from Wordsworth, entitled 'Upon Westminster Bridge':

> *Earth has not anything to show more fair:*
> *Dull would he be of soul who could pass by*
> *A sight so touching in its majesty:*
> *This City now doth like a garment wear*
> *The beauty of the morning: silent, bare,*
> *Ships, towers, domes, theatres, and temples lie*
> *Open unto the fields, and to the sky,*
> *All bright and glittering in the smokeless air.*
> *Never did sun more beautifully steep*
> *In his first splendour valley, rock or hill;*
> *Ne'er saw I, never felt, a calm so deep!*
> *The river glideth at his own sweet will:*
> *Dear God! The very houses seem asleep;*
> *and all that mighty heart is lying still!*

We were taken to see the film Hamlet, which starred Laurence Olivier. Another school outing was to the Last Night of the Proms at the Royal Albert Hall when the famous Sir Malcolm Sargent was the conductor.

In history lessons we learned about the Ancient Egyptians, Greeks and Romans as well as mediaeval and modern British history, but we were not taught anything about the two world wars. Our parents had lived through both, and we the second, so we never thought of them as 'history'.

The Sixth-Formers had a period called Current Affairs. We weren't interested in politics, but I did sometimes think how different everything had become in such a short time. I had been brought up to be fiercely patriotic, when Great Britain had been the leading global power and was alone confronting the Enemy; with first a reluctant Communist Russia finding herself on our side, then big, industrialised America stepping in to join the fight for freedom.

Now, in just a few years, our leading role in the world had been taken over by the USA; and the Americans, British and French were trying to restore our former enemies, Germany and Japan, to functioning states run on the lines of Western democracy.

Along with the USA, Germany and Japan would eventually become the world's largest economies.

At the same time, two of our wartime allies, Russia and China, had become new enemies, confronting us across the new divide between West and East.

When China fell under Mao's Communist regime, a flood of refugees poured into the British territory of Hong Kong.

18. Another New Word, 'Teenager' ~ 1949/50

At last Tadek found employment where he could use his scientific qualifications and Barbara managed to find a flat in Enfield, so they were finally able to get married in the spring of 1949 at St Andrew's Church in Enfield Town. I was the bridesmaid and Tadek's friend Adam the Best Man. We held the Wedding Reception at home in the garden and Barbara and Tadek left to travel by train to Switzerland for their honeymoon. I was envious – the practice of going on holiday abroad was only just beginning.

Before the war, only the minority who could afford it had crossed the channel to visit Europe. Even fewer had the opportunity or money to pay for a passage or cruise on the great liners across the oceans. All this changed with the rapid growth of travel agencies and airlines. Later, with the introduction of 'package' holidays, increasing numbers of people began to spend their holidays abroad.

As a consequence, shipping lines declined, along with our shipbuilding industry. In Britain's bankrupt state, this was the beginning of a more general decline in which many of our industries, such as motor-cycle manufacture, were taken over by other nations.

Barbara and Tadek visited Vienna during their honeymoon. Vienna was notorious as a place full of spies so, of course, when they came back, Barbara had more funny stories to tell. She said that every time they went to a café for morning coffee there would be a small group of shady-looking characters in trench coats with trilby hats pulled down over their eyes, sitting in a corner and muttering together. She swore that every few words she heard 'Fumph' – the name of the sinister German spy character in the wireless comedy, 'ITMA', who was always telephoning Tommy Handley to threaten him in a strong foreign accent!

Frank moved into Barbara's room and used it as his studio, while I moved back to my own tiny bedroom, which Frank had been using. Occasionally I gave Frank some help when he had too much to do –

my job was to brush on pale water-colouring on the background of some parts of his architectural drawings.

The BBC News these days was all about what was going on in the Cold War.

Early in 1949, the North Atlantic Treaty Organisation, NATO, was established as a defence against Soviet aggression and in June 1949 the Russians finally had to give in and lift the Berlin Blockade, but they made it clear they would never allow Germany to become united again. The British, French and American Zones were combined to become one Western Zone. The same happened in Berlin, which was divided into West and East.

Germany had become two states: democratic West Germany and the Soviet People's Republic of East Germany. Movement of people from East to West Berlin eventually became a flood as they tried to escape Soviet domination. This situation would last until 1961, when the Communists erected the Berlin Wall and posted sentries to guard it and to shoot anyone trying to escape into West Berlin.

My school friends and I acquired a taste for the theatre. We went up to the West End by trolley-bus and queued up for cheap seats in the 'Gods' (the Gallery) for the Saturday matinees: 'Ring Round the Moon' with Paul Scofield; 'A Street-Car named Desire' with Vivien Leigh; or Shakespeare plays whenever Laurence Olivier, John Geilgud or Ralph Richardson appeared.

You had to make sure of arriving very early to get into the Gallery. It was a matter of 'first come, first served' and the theatre management provided rows of small canvas stools, three or four abreast, for the long queues, which trailed along the pavement and sometimes around the corner.

After the play was over we waited at the Stage Door to waylay the actors and collect their autographs on our theatre programmes. On one occasion it was Laurence Olivier who hurried out of the Stage Door and my friend Catherine and I accompanied him up the side alley while I listened, amazed, to my self-assured classmate chatting merrily to him, even going so far as to congratulate him on his performance! Catherine had ambitions to be a theatre critic and I supposed she already saw herself in this role.

A smart black limousine waited at the end of the alleyway where it joined the main road, with Vivien Leigh *(then Olivier's wife)* sitting in the back and, to our delight, this goddess of stage and screen smiled and said hello to us. We collected both of their autographs, which I added to my collection.

We were still going to the pictures regularly. Most families could not yet afford television and it was Hollywood's heyday. In contrast to the British film industry, which lacked the money, Hollywood was turning out a stream of good films.

Some Hollywood films about the war reinterpreted actual events to make them more popular for an American audience. However, a film about the Burma campaign, depicting it as an American action, caused such outrage in the UK that it had to be withdrawn after a week. Another film, 'The Bridge over the River Kwai', brought in a fictitious American operation so that American actors could take part. Hollywood has produced many good war films, but some of them depict British exploits with American actors, giving a distorted impression of history to modern audiences.

Dad told me that film-makers interpreted history freely for the sake of dramatic effect, but in the Soviet Union history was rewritten deliberately for reasons of propaganda. After the Russian Revolution, the Soviet-approved version of history was taught in schools so that the next generation would grow up with government-approved attitudes, including hostility to Western ideas of freedom and democracy.

Some of the films shown became classics, such as: 'Gone with the Wind', starring Vivien Leigh with Clark Gable; and 'Oliver Twist' with Alec Guiness as Fagin. Another film starring Vivien Leigh was 'Caesar and Cleopatra', based on the play by George Bernard Shaw, with Claude Rains as Caesar.

There were quite a few American gangster films with stars such as George Raft or James Cagney; and American cowboy films with John Wayne and Robert Mitchum. And the famous Humphrey Bogart and Katherine Hepburn appeared together in 'The African Queen'.

Every year in summer, as well as a Sports Day, the school held a Swimming Gala with races and diving competitions. There were also life-saving classes. I passed a test, 'saving' someone pretending to be drowning – who clutched at me until I nearly went under myself – and gained a Bronze Medallion engraved with my name from the Royal Life-Saving Society. My friend Jenny and I bought season tickets for the open-air swimming pool so that we could go there any day to practice.

On Speech Days at the end of summer term, the Headmistress handed out prizes (books) for Good Work and we all sang the school song, 'Jerusalem'. I had what was called a 'gift' for languages, usually coming top of the class in English, French and Spanish exams and, in July 1949 at the end of my fourth year, I received a prize for the third (but last!) time.

At home the neighbours still dropped in to talk to Mum and Dad. The conversation often turned to the 'Arms Race'.

The Americans, with the British 'Brain Drain', were continuing to develop nuclear weapons. Russian scientists, informed of Western scientific research by their spies, determined to catch up with them. In August 1949, Russia detonated its first atom bomb and the Arms Race began.

All anyone could do about the threat of 'the Bomb', hanging over the world like the Sword of Damocles, was to try not to think about it – but it was hard to forget it!

In the summer holidays Jenny and I went on long bike rides. From Enfield Town centre it was only about 15 minutes ride to get into the open country.

This was long before the circular M25 was built around London. In those days, even on the main roads, it was not difficult to cycle alongside the traffic. According to National Statistics - Social Trends, there were only four million privately owned cars in the 1940s compared with over 30 million today. There were no seat belts, no speed limits, no parking restrictions, but drivers had to obey the Highway Code, which ensured good driving manners and safety precautions.

Jenny and I set off early one day to cycle to Bath, going along the North Circular Road until it reached the Great West Road leading out from Hammersmith as far as the open country. About halfway on our journey, an army lorry full of young soldiers on National Service picked us up, bikes and all, and gave us a lift for 40 miles. We stayed at the youth hostel and visited the Roman Baths.

Another time, we hitch-hiked to Dover and back again. Lorry drivers had become used to giving lifts to individual servicemen during the war and they continued doing this for penniless students. *At that time hitch-hiking was not as risky as it became later.*
We also enjoyed camping. Once we cycled to Walton-on-the-Naze with our camping equipment packed on the bikes, and put up our little tent in the corner of a field. In the morning the farmer brought us a couple of fresh eggs for breakfast.

Mum, who was getting fed-up with Frank mournfully playing 'Among My Souvenirs' on the piano, persuaded him to take me to my first dance, hoping he would meet a new girlfriend. Young people went to dances to meet someone new – only *old* people went to pubs!

Frank took me to the Southgate Ballroom and taught me, in quick succession, how to waltz, foxtrot and quickstep. My brother then abandoned me to try his luck elsewhere and I had to sit with the 'wallflowers' waiting for someone to come up and ask for a dance. There was always a Last Waltz at the end of the evening, when it was traditional for your partner to take you home, so I sought out my brother to rescue me from the unwanted attentions of someone I considered much too old – he must have been at least 25! Frank was a bit fed-up but, after all, he had to look after his little sister. The dance ended with the band playing the National Anthem and everyone standing to attention.

A week after my 15th birthday I started my fifth year at school. It was time to prepare for School Certificate *(a somewhat higher grade than the later O'levels)*. It was during this fifth year – the most important – that my work became rather erratic. The new experience of being called to the telephone for social events was a total distraction from studying. Another new word 'teenager' was now in vogue – and teenage gatherings at Jenny's house took up the time I should have spent on homework.

Some of my favourite evenings were spent at Alexandra Palace, where there was a huge roller-skating rink. I cycled there to join my friends, wearing what we called jeans or pedal-pushers – trousers cut short at calf-length. *(Blue denim jeans had not yet made their appearance in the UK.)* We could compete in races around the edge of the rink, or join in the skate-dancing when popular music records were played.

I was invited with Jenny to a Jazz Club in Enfield, where Chris Barber and his band were playing. *(This was before Chris Barber became famous.)* Most of the jazz fans just sat and listened reverently, but we joined in with the few who seemed to know how to jive!

I had grown out of my old green winter coat and a new one was out of the question. Once again Mum came to the rescue. She cut material from another worn-out coat of darker green, and added a 15-inch deep false hem and deep false sleeve-cuffs to my old coat which had a 'flared' skirt. This transformed it into the fashionable 'New Look' (the postwar style created by the famous Parisian fashion-designer Christian Dior), which I wore with something of a swank.

Dad played his part by mending everyone's shoes. He had his own cobbler's last (a piece of cast iron, shaped like the sole of a shoe), fixed to a bench in the garage, over which he fitted the shoe for repair. The garage was his workshop – it never housed a car. By this time he had demolished the Anderson shelter and he positioned the iron arches of its framework at intervals over a grassy track through our little vegetable plot at the bottom of the garden. Every year he grew a fine crop of runner beans to climb over them.

- *NEWS: War in Korea! (June 1950)*

At the end of the war with Japan, the Soviet Union had taken control of the northern part of Korea, while the southern part was taken over by the US military. In June 1950, communist troops from North Korea invaded South Korea. The United Nations responded and troops from the USA, Britain and several British Commonwealth countries were sent to defend South Korea.

The Cold War had turned hot only five years after the end of the Second World War.

I had other worries on my mind. The School Certificate exams were drawing closer and I knew I'd have to hurry up and do a lot of hard work. Along with other fifth formers at the end of the school day, my friends and I gathered in the Lyons Tea-Shop in the high street for chocolate cup-cakes and cups of tea. Then we went on to do 'revision' work in the reference department upstairs in Enfield Town Library, until it closed at 10 o'clock.

Most exams were split into two or three parts, each lasting one or two hours. They filled every morning and afternoon for two weeks, with every evening spent revising in the library. I'd always been good at exams – by dint of last minute swotting – and hoped for the best. However, on Speech Day, before the exam results were known, I was mortified when my name was not read out on the list that year for a Good Work prize. So much for my teenage social life!

Later that summer I received the results of the exams by post and was relieved that my hard revision had paid off. I gained exemption from Matriculation with credits in eight subjects and distinction in French and the school expected me to go on to the Sixth Form to prepare for Higher School Certificate *(later replaced by A-levels)*.

I was not sure about the future. I felt I'd been a schoolgirl long enough. My friend Jenny was leaving school to take a college art course at Hornsey School of Art. Others too were leaving and I seemed to be the only one undecided about the future. Along with Jenny I'd passed the entrance exam to the art college, thinking I might follow in her footsteps. But in the end I was persuaded to enter the Sixth Form – and found I could attend a part-time Saturday course at Hornsey, where I was to meet a whole lot of different students and become temporarily as 'arty' as they were.

In the summer holidays I received an exciting invitation from my cousin Clement, now a school headmaster, who had founded a small film company with a friend Hugh *(brother of the actress Hermione Baddeley)*, to make educational films for schools. He asked me to take part with one of my friends in a new film he was making, called "Using the One-Inch Map." Barbara had already 'starred' in one of his history films as a Georgian lady.

Jenny and I went along 'on location' (as Clem put it, to our delight!) in the South Downs, near the Devil's Dyke. *Today, a plaque there refers to John Constable saying that this was the most beautiful view he had ever seen.* We stayed in Brighton and drove out every day for filming. Clem and Hugh followed us with their cine-cameras while we 'acted' at poring over the map, pointing to a distant landmark, slithering down steep wooded slopes, and so on.

We enjoyed ourselves immensely and were later delighted to know that the film had been shown, praised and even chosen to be buried in a time-capsule "underneath Shaftesbury Avenue" according to Clem. The unusual thing about this film was that it was made in colour, which was very new and expensive. *(Much later in life, when I asked for a copy of the film from the National Film Institute, I received only a black-and-white version – the colour had faded over the years. Britain lagged behind both Germany and the USA in developing good colour film, presumably because of our state of bankruptcy at the time.)*

19. A Visit to Franco's Spain ~ 1950/51

In the Sixth Form, I continued with English, French and Spanish. My class also included those taking Latin and/or Ancient Greek and we split into groups for our different subjects.

Several of my classmates had their sights set on Higher School Certificate as a prelude to Oxford University, but as neither my sister nor my brother had gone to university I was not expecting to go myself. I knew my parents could hardly afford it. For them it was more a question of when I could start work and contribute to my keep! *(Just for the record, my sister later studied as a Mature Student and took a degree in geography; and my brother, also in later life, achieved the Final in his architectural exams.)*

I had made a special friend of the Spanish teacher and she offered me the chance of going to San Sebastian to attend the Summer School of Spanish Language and Literature. This trip was being organised for selected schools, one pupil from each, by Professor Allison-Peers of the University of Liverpool.

My parents were horrified when they found out the cost – £40 for a month staying with a Spanish family, £11 return train fare, £10 pocket money. Mum declared it was out of the question. *(My parents had never heard of school trips abroad – they weren't usual at that time.)* Dad's only trip to foreign parts had been his expedition to Flanders in the First World War and my mother had never set foot beyond our shores.

I pleaded and bullied by turn, backed up by my teacher, until my parents gave in. I supposed Dad must have run up a bit more of his overdraft – he was always talking about his overdraft! – but all I cared about was the chance to travel abroad for the first time in my life.

Now I was even more impatient to leave school uniform behind and join the world of college students, who could wear what they liked. A grammar school and college education was the respectable alternative to university, which was then mainly for those intending to take up a profession such as law, medicine or architecture, or one of the sciences. *It was not until decades later that many colleges were re-named as universities to upgrade the courses they offered to degree level.*

A tentative proposal of mine to study full-time at the art college was met with strong discouragement from my practical parents. "What sort of job can you get afterwards?" The Headmistress intervened. "Pat should not waste her language ability." She proposed the Institut Français in South Kensington which, apart from the school for children of French families living in London, offered a one-year French secretarial course to English students, starting in September.

Unable to decide what to do with my life, I settled for this as the shortest route to financial independence. I was too impatient to consider my Spanish teacher's disappointment in me when she found I wasn't even coming back to school, after the trouble she had taken to arrange for me to visit Spain.

In the spring I went with my parents to the Festival of Britain. This was opened by the King on 3rd May 1951 to commemorate the 100th anniversary of the Great Exhibition at Crystal Palace – a celebration of the achievements of British scientists, engineers and inventors. The exhibition pavilions, set out on the south bank of the Thames, included such wonders as the 'Dome of Discovery', 'Space and Astronomy', 'The Modern Home' and other displays by the best British manufacturers with the emphasis on science, design and technology.

We spent a whole day there. We admired especially the Skylon, a 300-foot high edifice erected as a symbol of the modern world. But we felt some misgivings when we saw the new Concert Hall built as a showpiece of Modern Architecture, which, in our view, was just a great expanse of concrete. On another day we visited the wonderful Funfair in Battersea Park Pleasure Gardens, which remained in place for several years.

The last poem we read at school was 'The Fox's Prophecy: Albion's Fate' by D.W. Nash *(written in 1870)*, which painted a depressing picture of the future:

For not upon these hills alone the doom of sport shall fall.
O'er the broad face of England creeps the shadow on the wall.
Time-honoured creeds and ancient faith, the Altar and the Crown,

Lordships' heredity right, before that tide go down.
Base churls shall mock the mighty names writ on the roll of time.
Religion shall be held a jest and loyalty a crime.
No word of prayer, no hymn of praise sound in the village school.
The people's education, utilitarians rule.
The homes where love and peace should dwell, fierce politics shall
     vex,
And unsexed woman strive to prove herself the coarser sex.
The statesman that should rule the realm, coarse demagogues
     displace.
The glory of a thousand years shall end in foul disgrace.
Trade shall be held the only good and gain the sole device.
The statesman's maxim shall be peace and peace at any price.
Her army and her navy, Britain shall cast aside;
Soldiers and ships are costly things, defence an empty pride.
The footsteps of the invader then, England's shore shall know,
while homebred traitors give the hand to England's every foe.
Disarmed before the foreigner, the knee shall humbly bend,
And yield the treasures that she lacked the wisdom to defend.

I was full of excitement when I met the other students at Victoria Station to catch the Boat Train (not, sadly for me, the luxurious Golden Arrow!)

After the ferry crossing *(no Channel Tunnel in those days)* we travelled overnight, sitting on the hard wooden seats of an old French train, as far as Irun on the Spanish border. The only way to sleep was on each other's shoulders. I made friends with another girl, Barbara, known as Bambi, who was going to stay with me in the same Spanish household. We were all glad to get out of the train in the morning under cloudless skies and a burning sun.

Coming from a country where we were used to kindly, unarmed 'Bobbies' on the streets, we were alarmed at the sight of the Spanish Customs officials, the Guardia Civil, who were all looking very fierce in military uniform with bristling moustaches and revolvers stuck in their belts. Seated behind an armoured glass partition (also then unknown in our generally law-abiding country) an officer examined my passport photo, looked up at me and, to my relief, smiled for the first time, muttered "Guapa, guapa" as a compliment and waved me through.

Another short train journey to San Sebastian and we set eyes on the beautiful bay between two small peaks with a little rocky island set bang in the middle, the long beach of golden sand, called La Concha, curving around it in a semi-circle.

The most intriguing part of San Sebastian for me was the Old Town with its narrow, cobbled streets and squares, leading away from the harbour, which was filled with fishing trawlers, rowing-boats and tiny sailing-boats. We had to attend classes every morning and there was homework to do, but after lunch and siesta we were free to enjoy ourselves.

One of the first things Bambi and I did was to swim out to a big white motor yacht moored in the bay. Sailors looked out of the portholes, laughing and waving at us. A police boat came along and shooed us away – and we were told when we got back that it was Franco's yacht and he was also on holiday!

The Spanish family with whom we were staying had solemnly warned us never to mention the name of the dictator Franco in public and it was then that we realised the Basque people were all very hostile to him. I supposed this was why so many armed Civil Guards *(Guardia Civil)* were always to be seen patrolling the streets.

However, this did not stop Bambi from asking the captain of Franco's yacht, when he came ashore in a magnificent white and gold-braided uniform, if she could take a snapshot of him. He agreed with enthusiasm and posed proudly in front of the low harbour wall, with the yacht in the bay as a background.

Another time we swam from the beach to the island in the bay and were given a free ride back on the island ferry, on condition we both plunged into the water a short distance before arrival at the quay, to save the ferryman's blushes when it was found we had no tickets.

We soon got to know the young 'marineros' around the harbour who invited us out on their boats for a trip or took us over to the little island. They were delighted to have the chance of taking us out, for they could not so easily approach Spanish girls, who were always chaperoned in public.

We discovered how strictly women had to behave when we were sunbathing in our swimsuits one day, lying on our backs on the beach. A policeman in white uniform came along and prodded us with his baton, telling us to turn over and lie on our fronts!

During the siesta, after a very late lunch at about 3.00 p.m., the streets were empty and everything was closed. Our Spanish hosts expected us to go to bed for a couple of hours, as they did. And we complied because it was so hot.

In the evening the town came back to life. Shops opened again for three or four hours and the evening 'paseo' began – an evening walk by all the population, with families and babies or young women walking together and the young men walking separately, eyeing the groups of women. Bambi and I were told by our Spanish hostess that this was the only opportunity for a young Spanish woman to spot a potential boyfriend under the chaperoning eyes of other women.

Cinema and theatre programmes started at 11 p.m.; and cafes and restaurants stayed open until 3 o'clock in the morning. If we came home late at night we had to clap our hands loudly three times to call the concierge to the front door of the building, for there was no bell to ring and the door was locked after 2.00 a.m. Our host family had an apartment on the first floor, with a little wrought iron balcony outside overlooking the square.

The Spanish family wanted us to go to the 'Corridas' (the bullfight). We were a bit doubtful, but they were insistent. Indeed, they said we hadn't *lived* until we'd seen the bullfight – and the most famous bullfighter in Spain was due to appear in San Sebastian! *(I forget his name but it may have been the famous Luis Miguel Dominguin.)*

At the last moment it was arranged. Escorted by the son of the family with his wife, we arrived at the bull-ring and found that all the seats in the shade had been taken. We had to sit on the hot stone (the seats were deep stone steps, packed with spectators) on the sunny side of the arena.

The Matador (bullfighter) was dressed in a bright blue, cream and gold costume of knee breeches and bolero, covered with sparkling jewels. The bull charged out of a corridor from one side of the arena. Before the fight proper began, the 'Picadores' (mounted on horseback with long, pointed weapons) jabbed and tormented the enraged bull until, at last, the Matador stepped forward to challenge him. He shook out his scarlet cape in front of him. Then began the death ritual between man and beast.

The bull charged, the Matador stepped aside at the last minute, again swept his cape around and again the bull charged. We were both fascinated and horrified while the crowd got more and more excited, yelling 'Bravo!' every time the Matador escaped death by inches with a neat movement like a ballet dancer. At last came the Matador's thrust with his spear. He had to kill instantaneously at the moment when the bull, stopped in mid-charge in front of him, was hesitating and bewildered. He leant over the bull's lowered head to pierce it through between the horns and the beast slumped down slowly in a pool of blood.

The dead body was dragged from the ring to make way for the next bull-fight, leaving us with mixed feelings of admiration for the toreador's skill and depression over the bull's death. Trying to make us feel better, our hosts told us that fighting bulls were given an extra year of life after other bulls had gone to the slaughterhouse.

After each bull-fight the Matador walked across the arena and bowed to the dignitaries sitting in an upper gallery and the crowd threw flowers to him and cheered.

What we enjoyed more were the displays of flamenco dancing which took place every evening in the main square of the Old Town. It was August, the time of the Basque Fiesta, and there was music and dancing for all the people in the streets every night. Neither Bambi nor I lacked for partners, who taught us the most popular dance, the 'Paso Doble'.

For me it was a month in Paradise. As the Spanish boys were eager to take out foreign girls, I learnt more Spanish during that month than in six years at school. I was even tactless enough to write home saying I wanted to stay there forever and got short shrift in a reply from my mother!

20. London Belongs to Me! ~ 1951-53

Back in England, still wistful about the romance and adventure I had left behind in Spain, I started my course at the French Institute – a daily journey by trolley-bus to Wood Green and a long ride on the tube to South Kensington. At the college we had to knuckle down to learning commercial French, book-keeping, touch-typing and shorthand in both English and French. I also continued to study Spanish.

Everyone had to speak French inside the college – this included making excuses in French if you were late or missed a lesson. Even Spanish was taught by a French teacher and translations, both verbal and written, had to be made from French to Spanish and vice-versa. I found a useful little French-Spanish dictionary at a nearby French bookshop in South Kensington.

Another General Election took place during our first autumn term and despite Dad's loyalty to the Labour Party I was secretly rather pleased when our famous war leader Churchill was reinstated. People were fed up with the housing shortage and continued rationing – even bread was still rationed – and hoped that Churchill would turn things around. At least, I thought, he would make a more interesting Prime Minister.

I soon found out that it was absolute bliss to be alive and 17 years old in London in the early 1950s. The bombing scars had become part of the landscape, along with the red buses, red telephone kiosks and red pillar boxes which, for me, made London so familiar and dear. It never occurred to me how modern architecture would change that familiarity. I only knew there was an excitement in the air, the feeling of new beginnings.

There were still vestiges of chivalry, with men showing respect for women by opening doors for them or giving up their seats in buses and trains. Out in the evenings we took for granted we were safe. In news reports of crime, women were rarely attacked and elderly people never. In this respect there seemed to be a code of honour, even among criminals.

If you got lost an obliging policeman was never too far away to show you the way. The conductor had a cheerful word as you boarded the bus. The roads were busy but car drivers could park, subject to the Highway Code, wherever they found a space. *There were no yellow lines, nor parking meters on the roads.*

Italian coffee bars were springing up everywhere, frequented by students of all nationalities. My college friends and I spent as much time as we could in this new Café Society, drinking coffee and arguing about 'the Meaning of the Universe' – flattering ourselves that we were reliving the Left Bank artists' community in Paris.

In our efforts to appear as interesting and sophisticated as the cosmopolitans around us, we started smoking, along with the coffee-drinking, as most people did at that time. *A pack of 10 Weights cost 1s.4d (16 old pence).* We were vaguely aware that smoking was not good for you, but even in hospitals the doctors, nurses and patients took for granted that they could smoke.

Medical opinion then was that it was not harmful so long as you did not smoke more than 10 cigarettes a day (we couldn't afford more than two or three a day, anyway) .

Sometimes a lone guitarist strummed in a coffee-bar, although generally music was played only in expensive restaurants. *A few years later, jukeboxes appeared in roadside and seaside cafés. Push in a shilling and choose your favourite record.*

By this time clothes had become more important. One of the fashions was a full circular skirt cinched in at the waist by a four-inch wide elasticated black belt with a big brass buckle. There was little money for new clothes. My mother spent even more time these days crawling about the living-room floor with material and paper patterns. At least it was easy to make a circular skirt – she just had to cut out a big circle of material and another small circle in the middle for the waistband.

- *NEWS: His Majesty King George VI has died peacefully in his sleep at Sandringham House.*

The official announcement from Sandringham, on 6th February 1952, was that the King had retired in his usual health and passed away in his sleep. He was aged only 56 but had been a very heavy smoker and suffered from a worsening lung condition.

Everyone was shocked and saddened. Princess Elizabeth was immediately proclaimed Queen. She was told the news of her father's death while she was away in Kenya with Prince Philip – staying in a treetops hotel that was actually built at the top of a tree! – and they returned home immediately. The BBC cancelled all programmes and played solemn music all day on the radio for several days until the funeral, which took place at St George's Chapel, Windsor Castle. The streets were again lined with the thousands of people paying their respects.

A couple of hundred yards away from our college was the School of Architecture of the Polish University College, originally set up for the Polish ex-servicemen who came to live here at the end of the war and later extended to take on their younger generation. We students got to know them in the Natural History Museum gardens, where we all congregated during our lunch break to sit on the grass in the sunshine. The Poles, exiled and homesick, had made South Kensington into their own world, with Polish restaurants and food shops; and Polish clubs, libraries and bookshops.

With the Polish students we explored London's patchwork of contrasting areas, each having its own special character and atmosphere: South Kensington with its museums and colleges; Charing Cross Road – a street of bookshops where, with no money to spend, we browsed the shelves, usually in Foyles, the most famous one; and Soho, with its foreign food shops and cafes, where you could always find a cheap and tasty meal – although Soho had a somewhat bad reputation at night! (*We didn't see any 'antisocial behaviour' or street violence; nor did we see any rubbish-strewn streets or homeless people sitting on the pavements; and we knew nothing about drugs.*)

In the City, we leant on the parapet of London Bridge, watching the green flow of the Thames and the barges moving ponderously downstream, or wandered round Leadenhall Market, tucked away among the banks and stockbrokers. I loved the unexpectedness of turning a corner in London to find a narrow cobbled mews, a street market or the odd square of green with trees and birds, a spot of the natural world hidden away in the hustle and bustle.

On occasion we took a bus as far as Hampstead, a picturesque 'village' on the heights which, we discovered, was a haunt for writers, actors and other 'Bohemian' characters. Here, at night, you could look out from a high point on the dark Heath and see the lights of London on the horizon.

We visited the art galleries and museums *(all free at that time)* and borrowed books from the American library in Grosvenor Square. We sometimes took a rowing boat out on the Serpentine in Hyde Park and on occasion visited the Polish Hearth Club in South Kensington's Exhibition Road, where you could have a meal or, in the evening, dance to a small jazz band.

Always ringing home to give excuses for being late, I used any of the sturdy, red, public telephone kiosks located in numerous sites around London, each conveniently provided with a neat pile of directories if you needed to look up a number *(vandalism was still rare)*. Drop in two pennies, dial, press button A for an answered call or press button B to get your money back.

This, of course, was long before the existence of call-centres, press-button menus and robotic voices. You could speak directly to the person you asked for; you could call any local railway station to find out times of trains from the man on the spot; and telesales calls to the home were unknown.

We often finished off the day in one of the coffee-bars along the Fulham Road, or in the Kings Road in Chelsea, known for its art students and antique shops. A new film, 'Singing in the Rain', was showing at a little Chelsea cinema and one day after classes we went off to see it, rounding off the evening at a late-night coffee-bar. I was very late getting home and got told off by Dad.

Above all there was my own special stamping ground, South Kensington *(somewhat changed today)*, where it first dawned upon me that my beloved London was the only place in the world I wanted to be. Romance had blossomed and my bright young student days were numbered as I was introduced to the University of Life. But that's another story (with apologies for the cliché.)

I started my first job in the City at the Banque de l'Indo-Chine, where everyone spoke in French and I had to use French shorthand. As one of the few English members of staff, I was given an extra task, re-writing reports written in fractured English by a Polish executive.

Hurrying along the streets in my lunch-hour, along with the 'City Gents' in their bowler hats and pin-striped suits, I saw groups of people leaning over the barriers around the huge bomb craters, watching builders at work laying foundations. All across London, unfamiliar concrete tower blocks were rising, dwarfing the remaining older buildings and church spires. At the same time some areas remained bleak waste ground, cleared of bomb rubble but with no building development for years to come. Places such as the areas around Old Street and Liverpool Street tube stations remained drab for many years with broken pavements and a general air of disrepair.

Britain was still responsible for the defence of the colonies and the Whitehall Report 1952 noted that, since WW2, Britain had continued to put capital investment into all the sterling Commonwealth countries, at the expense of ourselves and at the expense of our own obsolete and outworn rail and road networks.

At last! Bananas were available again! I picked up a bunch nearly every day from a city market on my way to work. The stallholder wanted to know how I got through so many bananas and I told him I never had time for breakfast!

Dad still worked at home, now with a part-time secretary. The milkman still made daily deliveries. Mum still shopped in the busy high street. The buzzwords of the day were 'Service with a Smile' and 'the Customer is always Right.' But around this time the first 'supermarkets' made their appearance.

In time, with the proliferation of supermarkets, shopping in the high street declined, along with the specialist knowledge and service given by small shopkeepers, which included the repair of shoes, tools or electrical items. Over the years, many individual cobblers, ironmongers and haberdashers closed down, along with butchers, fishmongers and bakers, changing forever the character of high streets throughout Britain.

One of the Polish students invited me to the Farnborough Air Show in September. This was the day when spectators would hear the sound barrier broken – two sonic booms as the plane reached the speed of sound. John Derry, the pilot who had broken the record, would be flying this new futuristic plane.

We waited in eager anticipation in the crowd at the edge of the runway, but it was all over in one horrifying second – the sudden arrival of the plane, the double boom, a third bang, a ball of fire. As the plane broke up, the two engines 'flew' on, one coming over our heads and crashing into the crowd on the hill behind us. We heard the sirens of the ambulances racing. At the same time another pilot ran like a madman to another plane and took off right away. In my dazed state I vaguely remembered the riding school's advice: if you fall off your horse you must mount again immediately before losing your nerve.

It seemed that the air display was continuing, but we were in no mood to stay. What had happened was especially horrific on this lovely sunny day in 'peacetime'.

The BBC reported that the De Havilland 110 jet fighter disintegrated on breaking the sound barrier, killing John Derry outright and showering the watching crowd with debris. 27 people were killed and 63 injured.

By this time some of our neighbours had purchased televisions (their advent had been delayed by the war). My first sight of live television was not until the following year *(1953)*, when we were invited by a neighbour to go round and watch the Coronation of the new Queen Elizabeth, with its magnificent pomp and ceremony. Thousands of excited people lined the streets to watch the long procession of royalty and heads of states from across the world, all with escorts on horseback, following the royal golden coach.

That same year, the newly crowned young Queen began her world tour of the Commonwealth countries, where she received a rapturous welcome from the crowds wherever she appeared.

The Coronation was exceptional daytime viewing, for regular programmes did not begin until the evening. The BBC was the only television broadcaster, so there were no advertisement breaks; instead there was sometimes an 'Interlude' when music was played.

When we finally acquired our own (black-and-white) television, family life was never the same again. Mum had been the 'Managing Director' of all the meal time arguments and laughter on which we thrived, but conversation came to a stop because nobody wanted to miss the start of the evening's entertainment. Everyone who was at home carried the food into the sitting room to eat while watching and nothing else got done in the evenings. *(I forget now whatever it was that we used to do, but the radio, unlike television, hadn't prevented us from doing it!)*

Neighbours stopped calling round in the evenings because it was considered 'bad manners' to interrupt a family's television viewing. As more families acquired televisions, 'going to the pictures' lost its appeal.

In later years, thousands of Dominion, Rialto and Regent cinemas across the country were shut down or turned into bingo halls.

Road traffic rapidly increased and someone invented a new word 'smog' to describe the choking autumn fogs, now heavily polluted with petrol fumes.

Wartime seemed a long time ago, as did childish dreams of bluebirds bringing peace and 'happy ever after'. Now it was 'the Bomb' which overshadowed all else; high tower blocks rising over the old London skyline; thousands of immigrants; jet aircraft; supermarkets; television; thoughts of the unknown future . . .

It was the 1950s and I had grown up, after all.

Looking Back

"Progress was all right, only it went on too long."
James Thurber, 1894-1961

In 1940 our own little island faced the threat of invasion and the loss of freedom, only narrowly averted by the reckless bravery of a few young fighter pilots in what became known as the Battle of Britain. For ordinary people at home, the Blitz and the continuing years of wartime hardships were, in the main, borne with 'bloody-mindedness' and humour; while the witty and belligerent 'bulldog' oratory of Churchill gave us confidence and saw us through.

At any rate, I was fortunate enough to enjoy a happy childhood at a time when the adult civilian population was living at high intensity, with the risk of injury, death or destruction from the skies, or the loss of a loved one fighting overseas, making normal everyday life all the more precious.

As I grew up in the postwar years and learned more about the world, I realised how fortunate we were to live in a free country where most ordinary people at that time could be trusted. You will have heard about back doors being left unlocked in earlier times. Probably not many today will remember a time when there were no barriers of reinforced glass or plastic between the general public and the person behind the counter in such places as post offices, ticket offices, emergency wards or other public buildings. You could walk right up to No.10 Downing Street – no street barrier, only the single unarmed policeman outside the front door. Also, historical records up to the 1950s show that football fans from opposing teams mingled together at matches with no more confrontation than shouted insults or banter.

Came rock-and-roll and the new youth culture and everyone had a great time throwing aside the perceived restraints of old-world manners and reticence, together with the principles and values of our parents' generation. We had no thoughts then of rising drug addiction, increasing crime or – a new phrase for my generation – 'anti-social behaviour'; nor did we foresee the relentlessly increasing number of restrictions, regulations and watching cameras.

My generation grew up through the Second World War; the end of Britain's historic role as Leading Power and World Policeman; and the dismantling of the British Empire. We lived through the tensions of the Cold War; the Swinging Sixties; the Permissive Society; a huge increase in immigration and a technological revolution.

We saw the end of the steam train era; the falling into disuse of little branch railway lines and canals; and the closure of small shops, branch post offices, pubs and churches in towns and villages, while the face of Britain was transformed by building development, motorways and multi-storey car-parks to accommodate ever-increasing population and road traffic.

And when we look back to our childhood and youth we remember the big band music on the wireless; the early-morning postman and milkman – even on Christmas Day; the friendly 'Bobby' on the beat – or on his bicycle; everyday courtesy, humour and common sense; and, above all, respect for individual privacy and freedom. These were all part of that beloved 'foreign country' of the 1940s, which a generation fought to save and for which hundreds of thousands sacrificed their lives.

Appendix I ~ Tadek's Story

Tadek never spoke to the family of his experiences during the war but over the years he did tell some of them to Barbara.

Tadek grew up in Warsaw and did his National Service as an army officer cadet in the Polish cavalry, which was at that time still using horses! In 1939, before the war started, he was doing post-graduate work as an analytical chemist in Posnan.

The German invasion from the west was rapid and Tadek was immediately drafted into the army on active service. As the Russians invaded from the east, he was taken prisoner by the NKVD (Soviet secret police). They took him to a prison camp somewhere far to the east. Some time later he was put with other Polish officers on a cattle-truck train going west to Katyn, deep in the Russian forest..

The Russians were rounding up all the Polish officers they could find (to be executed as part of the Soviet policy of exterminating all educated and professional people to make a clean sweep for the Workers' Paradise).

Tadek managed, with another prisoner, to hack out a hole in the bottom of the truck. When the train halted for a while in snowdrifts, they both dropped through to the ground and dug themselves into the snow until the train moved on.

Later, at Katyn, 22,000 bodies were discovered with their hands tied behind their backs with wire and shot in the back of the head. At the end of the war, the Russians denied this massacre and tried to pin the guilt on the Germans, but the truth was finally revealed publicly in the 1970s.

During the long, dangerous and difficult journey south-west across occupied Europe, Tadek was recaptured, this time by the Germans, and taken to a prison camp in southern Germany.

Talking to Barbara, Tadek once compared the two prison camps. The Russian guards, he said, were reasonable, but the conditions appalling; the German camp was clean and efficiently run, but the guards were brutal to prisoners from the east – it was there he lost a number of teeth. He related one incident. A very senior officer visited and afterwards conditions greatly improved. News came later that this officer was a Pole who had infiltrated into the German army. He was shot as a spy.

Tadek escaped from the prison camp in Germany one night during an air raid. It took him days to get to France, hiding by day in barns and cornfields and travelling by night. As soon as he crossed the French frontier he took a chance, as he was in desperate need of food and water, and went to a farmhouse. The family hid him until contact was made with members of the Resistance.

In France, on the way to Paris, Tadek was able to hide in 'safe' houses indicated by the Resistance, who supplied him with forged papers that got him through security checks and German guards. In Paris the resistance workers provided him with addresses of people in the south of France who could help him escape into Spain. He finally took his chance on a train going south. His forged papers were good enough to get through the security checks on the train.

Finally Tadek was successful in making contact with someone willing to guide him over the Pyrenees. The guide travelled with him as far as Andorra. Tadek's feet were so badly blistered by this time that he could go no further. They took shelter in a farm, where a woman sewed up the breaks in his skin with an ordinary needle and thread which she dipped in boiling water.

When they continued their journey they had to hide from German patrols in the mountains, but the guide was skilful and they crossed the border into Spain. Here he was interned by Franco's Government at a camp called Miranda, until he was finally released to the British authorities in Gibraltar and taken by ship to Scotland to be debriefed.

Some years after the war, Tadek and Barbara visited Paris to try and locate the safe houses where Tadek had been sheltered. One of them was the home of a butcher who supplied meat to the Gestapo (Nazi secret police). Tadek was unable to find the places where he sheltered – he told Barbara that he had only entered or left them during the hours of darkness – but he did recognise the building that had housed the Gestapo.

Several years later, he and Barbara took a holiday to Scotland hoping to find the house where Tadek was debriefed, which Tadek described as very large with an estate. Again they were unsuccessful

– Tadek could not recognise any of the big houses they visited. However, there must be a record somewhere.

In later life Tadek had frequent nightmares. These began after the family watched a television documentary about the Warsaw Rising. Tadek died at the relatively early age of 62.

Appendix II ~ A Word on the British Empire

Our Monarch was Head of State of thirty-two nations of the British Commonwealth, today called simply 'the Commonwealth', and is still today Head of State of sixteen Commonwealth countries – with a few small islands unwilling to lose their status as British Crown Protectorates.

However, the most significant legacy of the 'Old World Order' is the widespread use of the English language and old British institutions as, for example, in India, where law and justice is based on that introduced by the British Raj; the army follows British traditions; and the railways are still running with the old British systems.

Lawrence James, author of 'The Rise and Fall of the British Empire' has written:

> "Contempt for the past is rooted in ignorance. The British Empire and those who served it deserve honour and respect. For all its mistakes and shortcomings – and yes, there were many – it remains what Lord Curzon called one of the 'greatest forces for good' in the history of the world. With varying degrees of sincerity, all Commonwealth states claim to respect democracy and standards of public conduct originating in Britain and integral to the Empire. For all [the Empire's] blemishes, it represented an ideal of enlightened public service."